D0252990

Golf Dads

BOOKS BY CURT SAMPSON

The Eternal Summer

Texas Golf Legends

Full Court Pressure

Hogan

The Masters

Royal and Ancient

Chasing Tiger

Five Fundamentals

The Lost Masters

The Slam

Centennial

Golf Dads

Golf Dads

FATHERS, SONS, AND THE GREATEST GAME

CURT SAMPSON

Houghton Mifflin Company
Boston New York 2008

www.houghtonmifflinbooks.com

Library of Congress Cataloging-in-Publication Data
Sampson, Curt.
Golf dads : fathers, sons, and the greatest game / Curt Sampson.
p. cm.
ISBN 978-0-618-81248-6
1. Golfers–Family relationships. 2. Golfers–Biography.
3. Father and child. I. Title.
GV964.A1S26 2008 796.3520922–dc22 [B] 2008001161

Printed in the United States of America

Book design by Lisa Diercks
Typeset in Monotype Bulmer.

MP 10 9 8 7 6 5 4 3 2 1

An earlier version of "Back to the *Mariposas*" first appeared in *Sports Illustrated.*

PHOTO CREDITS: page 19, Courtesy of Joan Rhoads; page 39, Courtesy of Getty Images; page 59, Courtesy of Colonial Country Club; page 79, Courtesy of David Feherty; page 95, Courtesy of Lynne Beechler; page 117, Courtesy of the Wolff family; page 139, Courtesy of Gay Jacobsen; page 157, Courtesy of Curt Sampson; page 177, Courtesy of the Burke family; page 195, Courtesy of Gilbert Freeman; page 206, Courtesy of Dan Strimple

In memory of Bob Sampson

CONTENTS

INTRODUCTION: Weldon, Byron, and Bob 1

1. REBIRTH DAY: Rick, Curtis, Kevin, and Ryan Rhoads 19

2. DADDY CADDIE: Byung Wook and Michelle Wie 39

3. $227.05: Ben Hogan and Marvin Leonard 59

4. ULSTERMEN: Billy and David Feherty 79

5. FORTY-INCH DRIVER: Doug and A.J. Beechler 95

6. CROSS-HANDED: Bill and Jeffrey Wolff 117

7. FAR: Erling, David, Peter, Paul, and Susan Jacobsen 139

8. DON'T HIT THIS CLUB UNLESS YOU'VE GOT FIVE HUNDRED DOLLARS: Lee and Daniel Trevino 157

9. OUR FATHER: Jack Burke Senior and Jack Burke Junior 177

10. BACK TO THE *MARIPOSAS*: Avery and Gilbert Freeman 195

ACKNOWLEDGMENTS 207

Golf Dads

INTRODUCTION

Weldon, Byron, and Bob

I tell you Julia, there's nothing so terrifying in the world as a son. The relation of father and son is the damndest, awkwardest . . .

—Thornton Wilder, *Our Town*

His clothes were impeccable, his manner purposeful, and his perfectly cut dark blond hair caught the sun just so. No one looked better at the pro-am, not even the pros, and no one seemed more at ease. He'd say a quiet something to Jack Nicklaus—inaudible to those behind the yellow gallery ropes—and Jack would smile and nod.

The handsome man with the enviable pairing loved being around the best players in the world, but Weldon Case was never much of a golfer. With a driver, he aimed fifty yards right, then, on his downswing, he lunged way left, as if stepping urgently on a bug—a My Way, fire-and-fall-sideways swing that offended the eye of purists, unless it amused them. "Sir, I'm sorry, I forgot your name," Tom Watson said to him once, shaking his hand on a first tee somewhere. "But I'll never forget that swing." They laughed. Where had they played together before? Was it Westchester or Palm Springs or Firestone? Had it been five years ago? And how are the kids?

Weldon Case's money came from hard work and telephones. How he built a tiny company in Hudson, Ohio, into a communications empire is partly explained by the title of a book he wrote in 1985: *Twenty-five Years of Dedication to Excellence.* Dedication to excellence required him to stay on the road for Alltel Corporation – he was CEO for Alltel and its predecessor, Mid-Continent, for twenty-five years – and to remember every name, shake every hand, and show the company flag at several big pro-ams every year. Weldon Case believed in the grand gesture: sometimes, when he came upon a subordinate's offensively cluttered desk, he'd sweep its surface with his right arm, knocking every file and tchotchke to the floor. His family noticed that when he took them out to dinner he often worked the room so thoroughly that they'd be looking at the dessert menu while his medium-rare New York strip sat cool and untouched on his plate.

"My dad had more best friends than anyone I've ever known," says his son Bill, an attorney in Columbus, Ohio. "But our relationship was kind of awkward. Ironic, because he seemed to have this fabulous relationship with everyone else in the world."

They mystified each other. Weldon Case sought out the best clothes from the finest tailors, and wore them like so many three-piece suits of armor. Bill's shirttails hung out. The CEO of Alltel attempted to enforce businesslike discipline in the home, but his son yawned or looked away and knew he couldn't get fired. Dad was driven; his boy sat in the back and fell sound asleep in the high school classes that bored him, which was most of them. Out of independence or defiance – certainly not from need – Bill earned his own spending money, joining the rough crowd of caddies at Lake Forest Country Club, earning $6 for carrying two bags around eighteen holes. Inveigled to take the entrance exam to Western Reserve Academy, an academically challenging prep school, Bill surprised himself by passing the test. But at a family confab he disappointed his father again by saying he didn't really want to go. After a few moments of theatrical silence, Weldon Case addressed his wife. "Our son," he said, "has just made the first of many compromises with mediocrity." The zinger worked; Bill went to the Academy, but only for a year, and at the cost of a little more distance.

"I was always a little tongue-tied around my father," Bill recalls. "It was rare to have a truly relaxing conversation with him. Especially you had to tiptoe around politics, Vietnam, and rebellious youth."

And hair – good God. Flowing locks on young males' heads reliably boiled Weldon's blood and caused him to wonder aloud *where* were those boys' *parents?* How could they allow their boys to look like girls? So when his own son let his see-through blond crewcut grow out into a cowlicky bird's nest, there was hell to pay at home.

Could this relationship be saved?

Yes.

What could save it?

Golf.

"Everything changed on the golf course," Bill recalls. "He was not an easy guy to get close to – for me, at least – but we communicated better when we played. Even 'nice shot' is communication. He could be complimentary about my good shots, even effusive."

The game leveled things, it seemed to Bill; it doled out humility to both of them, although he thought his father needed it more. Bill practiced hard and improved rapidly; at age thirteen, after only three years with a club in his hands, he began to beat his dad in their twice-monthly game. He read and absorbed Herbert Warren Wind's *The Story of American Golf* and both the big monthlies, *Golf Magazine* and *Golf Digest.* His handicap plunged to five. He made the high school golf team and even organized a summer tournament, the Hudson Junior Invitational. Once, Weldon took his son to New York, a trip that included dinner aboard his yacht with Cary Middlecoff, a friendly, alcoholic pro from Tennessee who'd won the Masters and the U.S. Open. And at Christmas one year, at the family's vacation home in Boca Raton, Florida, Bill opened an envelope with a message inside: "You have a game of golf tomorrow with Sam Snead." Weldon had paid Snead $200 to play golf with his son.

"We played in about two and a half hours, and Sam let me hit first so that everyone we played through would think I was kicking his ass," Bill recalls. "Snead could be a crusty character, as you know, but we got along fine because I'd read his book and could ask intelligent questions about his career." Sam shot 66, Bill, 82. But an even grander adventure awaited.

As a gift for graduating from high school, Weldon sprung for a trip to Scotland. For a week the Ohioans played the fierce courses at Troon, Gleneagles, Turnberry, and St. Andrews, with salt air and the smell of history in their noses. They ate dinner together every night, and there was no old friend or new client to take Bill's dad away from the table. But the single best moment of the best trip of Bill Case's life occurred on the seventeenth on the Old Course, the Road Hole, the most famous hole in golf.

The tee shot on the Road was a tricky thing. It was the one stroke likely to define the day, and the only specific shot anyone was likely to ask about back in the United States. But Weldon mistimed his awkward pirouette of a swing, and drilled his tee shot into the ancient railroad storage building that marked the corner of the dogleg. Bill giggled when the ball impacted the old lumber like a rifle shot, and he laughed delightedly when they discovered that Pop's Maxfli had imbedded in the shed like a marble in mud. Weldon's caddie had to pry it out with his strong fingernails.

The years went by after that, and the hard-charging father and his no-charging son continued to approach work and life from opposite directions. But, gradually, their relationship mellowed, and their rounds of golf together became deeply satisfying. Slowly, time made father and son a little more like each other: Weldon's life slowed down, while Bill went to law school, got a job at a big firm, and argued cases that were written about in newspapers and law journals. He won a particularly significant sex discrimination suit in 2006, *Vickers v. Fairfield Medical.*

They played one last time in August 1999.

Among his several vacation properties, Weldon had a home along the second fairway at Birchwood Farms Golf and Country Club, a way upscale community in Harbor Springs in way northern Michigan. He'd been ill – his heart – so Bill accepted his father's invitation to visit, and probably to say goodbye, not expecting that golf was on their agenda.

"The first day I was there, he saw I was going out to play, and he says he'd like to ride along in the cart and watch," Bill recalls. "And I said, 'Are you sure you can even do that?' He'd been spending most of his time in bed, and he'd lost a lot of weight. Then, when I got to the first tee, I saw that his clubs were on the cart too.

"I didn't think he could make it. He could hardly move. I was literally driving up on the tees because he couldn't handle even a small uphill step. I helped him out of the cart, teed his ball up for him, and handed him his club. And the damnedest thing happened."

It was a dreamy interval, like the scene from *Caddyshack* when The Bishop, played by actor Henry Wilcoxon, shoots the best round of his life during a blinding rainstorm, then is hit by lightning as he holes out on the eighteenth green. Weldon Case's final round was no less miraculous. Too weak for his usual step-in-the-bucket stroke, he had to whack the ball with his feet planted, an orthodox approach he'd tried and discarded many years before. *And he started flushing every shot.* Although he couldn't swing very fast, the center of his club found the equator of the ball with Hogan-like consistency and a pleasing tick-tock rhythm. On the seventh hole of the Farms nine, a 158-yard par three over a pond to an elevated green, Mr. Case nailed a driver, chipped indifferently, then, as Bill cheered, he holed the thirty-foot putt for a par. The third-to-last hole of his life; he died the next month, in September 1999.

And this is his son's last and most lasting memory of his father. Not the insignificant conflicts over hair or shirttails or the inevitable miscommunication between a successful executive and his adolescent son. No: when Bill Case thinks of his dad, he remembers the warm fellow feeling of playing a game together, especially their final game – and that ball stuck in the side of the storage shed at the Road Hole.

This is a book about fathers, using golf as a wedge to pry open a few insights.

Why golf? Let's see . . .

A couple of times I've imagined the torch passing when another game – say, hockey – animates a household, and a creaky-kneed dad on dull blades demonstrates how he used to fore-check or stickhandle. A football father might simulate in super slo-mo the way they used to trap block or cover a punt – I've seen this. Another class of dad shows off the leaden ballet of his jab step/jump shot, which gravity has devolved into a hop shot – I've done that. The kids watch, and wonder how to react.

What the child of an aging athlete *doesn't* see is his father getting on the phone to twenty-one of his friends to say, "Let's get the helmets and the pads and three officials and a defibrillator and line the field and play some damn football on Saturday!" Except in a diminished or instructional way, dads don't do soccer, hockey, football, baseball, or basketball. Those sports are for children or – sometimes – young adults.

Golf is different. Golf is as adult as single malt scotch. Golf is rated R. Golf is a striptease with no music and years between dropped garments. When a father introduces the game to his child, he's opening a window to himself and to the world of adults. The introduction is as valuable as good genes or a trust fund because golf is something to *do* and a golfer is someone to *be*.

It's a culture, in other words, not just a game. It's what to say and when to say it, and where to stand and how to act, and how to control yourself despite the most fiendish provocations, and how to do about a hundred other things to make the day pleasant for the others in your group even though you're playing like a monkey on crack. Guides to all this occult Scottish ritual are advised if not actually mandatory. And who guides better than a dad?

But when father keeps the game to himself too much and too often, golf becomes a dark force. If the family man's master problem is how to distribute himself between work, play, and family, and he stands in his spikes and a cardigan for entire weekends at the club, and he comes home only when they've run out of gin or he's run out of the capacity to drink it – well. The corollary to the golf widow is the golf orphan. At a funeral in Philadelphia, the daughter of the deceased addressed one of her father's buddies from the club. "I wish he'd spent as much time with us as he did with you," she said.

Not that taking a four-hour, five-mile hike around the links with one's children guarantees anything but exercise. Indeed, golf often provides a brightly lit stage for competition and control battles that might otherwise remain interred. Maybe it's good to get this stuff out in the open. Who knows? Either way, the game possesses no magic to make the generations feel peace and love, kumbaya.

For example: a popular New England club pro I know infuriated his father so acutely during one of their rounds thirty years ago that the dad felt compelled to grab his child roughly. But his hand slipped. It hit the golf cart's steering wheel, breaking his thumb, yielding a reliably hilarious family story told after holiday dinners, over wine. And out of the hearing of the father, who doesn't see the humor.

And another example: San Diego has many golfers and golf courses. It also has a United States Marine Corps base nearby, Camp Pendleton. The Marines have drill instructors, some of whom become fathers, some of whom play golf. One DI I met while researching this book virtually memorized *Play Better Golf with Hale Irwin* and decided to teach it to his son – the Marine Corps way.

It didn't work. His child began to hate the game his father gave him, and he resented that the family spotlight always shone on him, while his sister stood forever offstage. Like a preacher's kid, he rebelled, with skateboards and beer and a so-what attitude. From age thirteen through eighteen he didn't pick up a club.

Then, oddly, it did work. As the boy left his teens, he tried golf again, and, suddenly, everything clicked. Rounds in the mid-60s were almost routine. He had a little career as a touring pro. His greatest joy, he says, and his future in the game, is teaching golf to children. Then – odd symmetry – his father turned pro, too. "Because of him," Senior says, "I learned that I'm not a bad teacher."

Golf and fatherhood does not mean chicken soup, even when the subject is Byron Nelson, and the temptation to sentimentalize rises like a flood. Golf's perfect gentleman never fathered a child – he was sterile, probably the result of childhood illness – but no one has ever been more golf's patriarch.

I last saw him on a cool gray day in December 2005 at his

cozy home on his ranch in Roanoke, Texas. He'd gone downhill in the seven months since I'd seen him. He was ninety-three now and aching. His second set of replacement hips had become so painful and ineffective that he was spending most of his day in a wheelchair, and lately his lungs were bothering him. But when his guests entered he took the oxygen cannula from his nose and put aside the raft of things people had sent him to autograph. "Everyone from here to yonder," Byron said. He held up two FedEx envelopes. "This one's from Florida. This one's from Mamaroneck, New York."

He shook our hands. One last time I was reminded that Nelson had at least one trait of a player in the NBA. But his huge right hand was soft now, and ivory, not tan. He hadn't swung an ax or a golf club in years.

We discussed some golf-specific subjects – yes, of his sixty-one tournament victories, he still felt, as he'd said before, that the '37 Masters was his most important win. Yes, he agreed, his incredible season of 1944 has been virtually ignored by history. He won nine times that year and was named Athlete of the Year by the Associated Press. Then he overshadowed '44 – and every other year in golf up to then except for Bobby Jones in 1930 – by winning eighteen PGA events in '45, including eleven in a row. The kind old man in the wheelchair had been a marvel.

We moved on to family topics. For years I'd been imagining young Byron as the rural Texas equivalent of Jakie Rabinowitz, the main character in the early motion picture *The Jazz Singer*. In the film, Jakie disappoints his devout parents with his fondness for performing popular music – instead of sacred music, as five generations of Rabinowitz family tradition demanded. The father disowns the son, the son changes his name, falls for a gentile, and, as Jack Robin, performs in dance halls and saloons—a mess. Byron's parents were no less orthodox than Jakie's—Church of Christ, not Judaism—and they were country people, with a dim regard for golf professionals, actors, and singers. But at age twenty, their boy turned pro. He came home to Fort Worth after his first tournament in Texarkana and told his parents what he'd done. Daddy didn't say much. But Byron had won $75, a small fortune in 1932, and that must have softened the blow.

"They didn't resist when I told them what I wanted to do," Byron recalled. "The golf pro was about like a servant back then, which they knew from reading."

But you became much more than a country club servant, one of the guests pointed out. Within a few years your name was in the headlines, and your face was in the newsreels. You traveled across the country, and to South America, and to England for the Ryder Cup, and you made some real money. It must have been hard for your folks to understand . . . What was it like to come home after winning the U.S. Open?

"They didn't make a big story over it," Byron replied. "They were happy I was getting a good reputation, and they were always happy that I was going to church."

In his autobiography *How I Played the Game,* Byron had written that his parents "always supported me, even though they didn't get much of a chance to see me play." His guest asked what this meant, exactly. How often were they in your gallery?

"Dad never saw me hit a ball in his life," Byron said. "Mother saw me hit one, at the World's Fair in New York."

Byron adored his father—"Daddy John was the nicest person

I ever saw," he said. But something in the firm, clear way he said, "Dad never saw me hit a ball" hinted at an old wound. Because don't all children want their successes observed by their parents? And what son doesn't want to be made a story over?

My own golf dad returned from the office every day, or from a business trip, and ritually walked into the closet by the front door. He'd take off his suit, and hang it up, then, standing in his wrinkled white dress shirt and rumpled white boxers, he'd pour a shot of Seagram's V.O. from a bottle he kept on an upper shelf, up there with his hats. Only then would he engage with any of the eight people waiting for him, his wife and seven children.

His customs and ceremonies fascinated us. He smoked a pipe. He ate steak virtually every night, "because of my gut," he said, meaning his digestive process, not his stomach, which was as flat as a table. In fact, he considered most people in the world to be overweight, or "fleshy." Although he was a well-educated man and a big reader, he usually spoke in a very spare style that bordered on being inarticulate, with whistles, grunts, gestures with the pipe, and code words with multiple meanings. "Ass," for example, held a cornucopia of nuance. The phrase "my ass" indicated incredulity. "You bet your ass" meant certainty. Someone with "no ass" lacked courage. An annoying person was a "pain in the ass" (why there?). He'd speak of someone "getting their ass off the couch" (or to work or out of bed) as if the rear end could be detached from the rest of one's corpus. "Sitting on your ass" was despicable – it meant you were lazy – but where else, how else, do you sit? And ass size was virtually a preoccupation, and fair game for comment. Big was bad.

When the conversation at our crowded dinner table focused on touchdown catches and no-hitters, a sort of golden light seemed to flow between my father and his oldest son. The other seven of us felt we'd ceased to exist, but the pleasure of these moments overwhelmed my father. "God*damn*," he'd say, and clank down his shot glass of brown whiskey on the yellow pine. Intense happiness.

Ohio State wanted my brother for football and baseball, but, alas, he couldn't handle the academics or the easy access to beer on High Street in Columbus. Back home in our little town in northeastern Ohio, the glow dimmed at the picnic table where we fought and laughed and ate our inevitable casserole. Then the fifth child, the third son, showed a significant proficiency in a new game. My father's magic light snapped back on again, but it looked different this time, because now it was directed at me. Always a generically loved child, I advanced now to favored son. My sisters and brothers sat outside the light and faded from view.

My father wasn't an imbecile living through his jockstrap sons and it wasn't as if he hadn't tasted athletic glory himself. As the captain and left fielder for the Northwestern University baseball team, and, before that, a three-sport player for Senn High School, Bob Sampson got headlines and his picture in the *Chicago Tribune*. But when his basketball team advanced to the finals of the city championship, and he looked into the stands for a square Scottish face like his own, he saw . . . nothing. My grandfather, a handsome man, a drinking man, rarely lived with – and seldom paid attention to – his wife and four kids. He worked for the *Trib* as a pressman, so he had to read the paper every day, and could have easily known where and when his son was batting third against Notre Dame. But he never went to a game.

While my father attempted to atone for his father, he struggled with another set of dark emotions. During World War II, he'd rained death and destruction on targets in Italy, Germany, and Bulgaria. In his chilly compartment behind and above the B-17 pilot, he peered through a sight and pressed the button that released the bombs. The bomber crew's mortality was astounding – on some missions a third or more of the men who flew out didn't fly back – but Dad somehow flew fifty combat flights, the maximum the Army Air Corps allowed. His survival was a fluke. He thought a lot about the dead – pilots, gunners, and navigators he played poker with, and those unseen people on the ground in Sofia, Ploeşti, and Essen. He reacted by marrying a Catholic girl who gave him seven children, and by loving them all as much as he was able, and with drink. His laser focus on whichever son was doing very well in sports was, I guess, part of his therapy.

Bob Sampson's own recreation was confined to eighteen holes every summer Saturday morning. He found three other guys willing to tee off, quite literally, in the dark – Mom had been alone with us all week, so Dad had to get home quickly to keep the peace – thus golf had to happen early, and fast. Mr. Roehrig and Mr. Starr always grumbled good-naturedly about the arrangement as they walked in the dew on the first fairway. I, the caddie, did not. Although leaving my bed at four-thirty or five was a hardship, I loved having my father to myself for a few hours, and I became a witness to the secret world of grown men.

With money made caddying, I bought my first club, a Sam Snead Blue Ridge pitching wedge with an indentation at the top of the handle called a Reminder Grip. I was hooked. I got good. But recalling my life from age fifteen through twenty-five feels like an unpleasant waking, when, as the poet says, "the soul shrinks from all it is about to remember." I can't forget the mixture of gratitude and irony I felt when I became first among equals of the seven sibs. Golf enveloped me, and it in turn enveloped the family – at least part of it, part of the time. My mother drove me to tournaments, even though she hated to operate our stick-shift Jeep station wagon for any trip longer than to the grocery store. The Jeep had no air conditioning; skin adhered to its blue vinyl seats in the summer heat. My younger brother carried my bag occasionally, and my younger sister shagged practice balls regularly. From behind trees or from three hundred yards ahead, my father watched. Dad was there when my opponent made the hands-around-the-neck choke gesture after I'd hit a couple of bad shots on the seventeenth hole of a tied match, and he and I jumped at the same time when I pitched in to win the hole and the match and, eventually, the tournament. He was there when I managed to lose the state high school tournament, and he took me home when I pooped my pants on the sixth hole of a casual round on our home course (bad tuna in Mom's casserole).

My siblings felt amused, neglected, or envious about all the attention I got. I tried not to notice. Instead I concentrated ever more deeply on myself and my game until they became the same thing. The stakes rose higher each year, since success meant a shot at the scholarship I needed to go to college. I practiced obsessively, in the manner of Ben Hogan, until my hands bled. I was no prodigy; I was a grinder, a grim, depressive golf machine.

Nursing my cuts and a martyr complex, I reacted very badly when my father suggested that girls were cutting into my practice time. The hell with you, I said to myself, this is *my* game and *my* life. We hardly exchanged a word during my final year in high school, and I kept my parents out of the loop as I decided which university to attend. I pictured myself, again, as Hogan or as Gary Cooper in *High Noon*: a proud, solitary hero succeeding against long odds. I was an idiot.

Only after I'd washed out for good as a touring pro five years after college did my relationship with my father become comfortable again. But the brother I'd deposed as Dad's Favorite sank into bitterness. His resentment of me remains palpable. Even now, thirty years later, he can hardly bring himself to shake my hand or look me in the eye.

On the one hand, the collaboration – if that's what it was – between golf, my father, and me succeeded: I got the scholarship I needed, an identity I needed even more, a brief stint as a professional golfer, and a longer career as a writer. On the other hand, we both paid a high price.

I think, in the end, it was worth it. Virtually every time I came home, if there wasn't snow on the ground, we got out clubs and walked around the backyard and hit seventy-yard shots at trees. Golf gave us the momentum to talk about important things as they came up. But most of the time we didn't say much. We didn't have to.

This is a book about children, and their fathers, and the game towering in the background. The stories herein cover the waterfront: a few are touching, a couple are disturbing, and I'm at a loss to characterize the two chapters about prodigies. We've got touring pros, dead heroes, locally famous club professionals, a TV announcer everyone knows, and a couple of protagonists you've never heard of.

Perhaps the common ground throughout is – and I hope this doesn't sound sappy – love. Love, I discovered, is more mysterious and maddening than it might ordinarily be when the participants in the drama have clubs in their hands and a ball on the ground.

1

REBIRTH DAY

Rick, Curtis, Kevin, and Ryan Rhoads

A brown two-door 1970 Buick LeSabre sped south on I-5, tracing the spine of California. Behind the wheel sat Rick, a slight man wearing contacts beneath his sunglasses. Beside him, Joan, his pretty, dark-haired wife, divided her attention between the road ahead and the hubbub in the back seat. Actually, the car had no back seat; it had been torn out in favor of a playpen, which Rick had bolted to the floor. Inside the padded enclosure, among blankets, teddy bears, an Etch-a-Sketch, a Slinky, and a handful of GI Joes, Curtis and Kevin Rhoads gibbered and played and drooled and slept. They were ages four and two, respectively. It was 1974.

"We had a two-bedroom apartment in Woodland [a Sacramento suburb] where you could always hear trains going by," recalls Curtis. "We were there some and on the road a lot. I know

above: THE RHOADS BOYS ON VACATION IN SCOTLAND.

it seems a quaint thing now, but the tour and the car were our life and our lifestyle." When Curtis fell off a jungle gym and gashed open his forehead, Joan rushed him to a hospital. Somewhere. Neither of them remembers where between the Andy Williams San Diego Open in January and the San Antonio Texas Open in November this occurred. A quick trip to the ER and twelve stitches in your child's *cabeza* was merely business as usual for what sportswriters used to call "golfing nomads."

Cars with clubs in the trunk virtually defined the tour for the first fifty years of its existence. Roads still ruled – not jets – when Rhoads played in the '70s. Caravans formed on Sunday nights for the long haul from, for instance, the parking lot at Silly Willow Country Club in central Mississippi to hotels near the next event in Tallahassee. The following Sunday night the convoy snaked north to Philadelphia; then, a week later, west to Chicago, and on and on into the future like a runaway train. As ever, golf pros carried tools for minor repairs and learned to handle blowouts and highway hypnosis and bad food and all the other hazards of life on a concrete strip. The cars had to be big, so partly to fulfill the wheelbase requirement and partly to finance her husband's rookie year, Joan sold her treasured white Pontiac Firebird. "That car had some *guts,*" Rick says with a smile and a touch of remembered regret. The newlyweds missed the way the 'Bird pinned your spine to the seat, but one bland Buick was all they needed or could afford.

"One time he left me in Tucson," Joan says. Rick was feeling flush enough, or fatigued enough, to fly to Miami for the next tournament. "He said, 'Just follow Ken Fulton.' Well, Ken Fulton liked to go eighty-five, and he didn't like to stop. I was like this the whole way." Joan extends her arms and widens her eyes, the frozen pose she held for two solid days across seven states.

But on their usual, less frantic cross-country drives, when the kids were napping or playing with GI Joe, the couple had time to think and to talk. Joan looked at the farms and fields rushing past and wondered why fate had surrounded her with males all her life. She had five brothers, no sisters. Now two sons and a husband, with another baby boy in her future. A schoolteacher and a nongolfer, she often posed blunt questions. "Why did you miss that putt on eighteen?" she'd ask. "Why did you hit it in the water on twelve?" Admits Rick, "I never had an adequate answer."

As the odometer spun, Rick mused aloud, and in his head, about the future. As good as he was – and he knew he could really play this game – his position on the tour remained tenuous. Like his brother Ron before him, he'd attended USC on a golf scholarship, and twice was named All-American. He turned pro and succeeded immediately. In the late fall of 1967, in the eight-round qualifying tournament to get a PGA card – an event so stressful that vomiting at the first tee was almost commonplace – he sailed through on his first try. Rhoads and the other newly minted tour pros – Bob Murphy, Deane Beman, and Marty Fleckman among them – were summarily extended invitations to play in a series of tournaments around the rim of the Caribbean. The first one was in Caracas.

"It's the only golf memory that gives me chills," Rick recalls. He shot 65 his first round as a touring pro, then hung around well enough the next three days to have a final-hole fifteen-foot putt to tie Alvie Thompson for first. When he made it, it was as if he'd killed the bull: the throng of Venezuelans around the green punched the air and screamed in Spanish.

The outpouring of emotion – his own and that of *los aficionados* – left Rhoads drained. But then something else happened to make the moment even more vivid. Al Besselink, one of the tour's legendary bon vivants – he once played the eighteenth hole at Colonial with a rose in his teeth – put his arm around Rhoads's thin shoulders: "He said, 'Calm down, slow down. Everything goes at your pace now.' It helped. I don't think I would have made contact with the ball in the playoff if Bessie hadn't talked with me."

Rhoads won with a birdie on the first hole. First prize was $3,000.

He never won again.

For most of the next decade he eked out a living in the middle of the pack, and strived and studied the unforgiving game, a quest that included a season toiling at Winged Foot, in suburban New York City, for Claude Harmon. Because of Harmon's wonderful reputation, a spot on his staff was considered the best club job in the country. Graduates of his program owned the credential to work almost anywhere and to teach almost anyone. Claude Jr., AKA Butch, taught at Winged Foot when Rhoads did, and later hit the big time as Tiger Woods's swing coach. But Rhoads didn't want to work at a club. He wanted to play.

Play. If ever a word was inadequate for its purpose, it's "playing" professional golf. As if constant travel and backbreaking hours on a practice tee are play. After hitting a couple hundred balls himself, Rhoads often extended his workday by studying more successful practitioners. He'd walk down the practice tee and park a polite distance behind one superstar or another, often Gary Player or Lee Trevino – "because they were little guys, like me" – and just observe. Eventually, Gary and Lee would wave Rick in to discuss what they were working on and to have a look at his swing.

His biggest year was 1973, when he won $16,120, good for 113th on the money list. The equivalent in today's dollars is about $125,000 – not poverty, but after expenses, not much. The magic phrase back then was "top sixty": the sixty leading money winners could compete in any tournament they wished. But those ranked in the purgatory of 61st on up had to either make the cut in the previous event or play in one-round qualifiers on Mondays to earn a place in the main draw. It was a brutal way to live. When Rhoads didn't shoot low enough on Monday to make the tournament field, he often participated in minor league "satellite" events, a concept the tour toyed with to give their unemployed pros a little something to play for. A *little* something: in one satellite, the Future Stars Classic in March 1972, he won eight bucks.

But still, Rhoads got rich. Travel with his wife and two young sons bound them to a degree they might not have achieved otherwise. And stories: memories of his life on the run are as good as gold. What Nicklaus said on the first tee at the L.A. Open (it was not endearing). How Sanders, the tour's Romeo, handled his women (carefully, but honestly). How he himself endured the tortures of the damned when his dependable fade devolved into a hook so big he had to aim north to go west. The advice from Lee Trevino, when Rick got near the lead at the Hartford but then hurried his way into some late bogies: "You can't watch yourself, but next time you feel the heat, just look at your shadow. You and your shadow were moving so fast you looked like Charlie Chaplin out there." What a novice caddie said to Art Wall, when the soft-voiced pro squinted at a green and asked how far it was to get home: "Man, I don't even know where you live."

One story, The Story, is painful. Driving cross-country on the southern route – alone this time, and now in a burgundy Impala – Rick pulled off I-10 in El Paso and parked on a side street. He got out of the Chevy and yawned and stretched, observing the orange mountains across the river in Mexico and smelling the dry air. He walked for a while, then jogged for a mile or two. Several happy dogs ran with him. Back in the car to resume the interminable journey to Florida, he discovered blood on his leg. One of the dogs had bitten him. Just to be safe, he stopped in the next town that looked big enough to have a hospital. Good thing you came in, the doctor told him. There's a rabies epidemic in El Paso.

The rabies cure is a lot less stressful and intense now, but the state of the art in 1975 involved shots of vaccine and immunoglobulin once a day for two weeks. Faced with the knowledge that the virus, if he had it, would travel slowly from his peripheral nervous system to his central nervous system and then to his brain and kill him, Rhoads got back in the car to continue his worst trip ever, stopping in general hospitals along the way for his shots. "You should have heard the buzzing in those emergency rooms when I said the word *rabies,*" he says.

Despite the shots and the stress, Rhoads somehow qualified for the Jackie Gleason Inverrary Classic, and was even close to the lead after shooting 71-69. But he felt sick that Saturday night as he went to the by-now familiar hospital in Fort Lauderdale. The docs there made no specific diagnosis, so he played on, but not well, staggering to the finish in 73 and 77. He tied for fifty-third, winning $559. The weary pro packed the car for Jacksonville and the next tournament.

Feeling awful, he quit halfway through a practice round that week and drove to the local hospital for his fourteenth injection. There was blood in his urine. The doctors admitted him, and, suspecting that the rabies cure had caused the internal bleeding, decided to forego the final shot. But that wasn't it; tests eventually revealed the presence of autosomal dominant polycystic kidney disease. Rhoads had the most common inherited life-threatening disease in the world. Common, yes; cure, no, the physician said in response to the obvious question. All we can do, he said, is treat symptoms, such as backache, headache, and high blood pressure. But it's a long-term problem, nothing to worry about now. You've got to concentrate on getting your blood chemistry right, and the only way to do that is to eat right and rest.

Rhoads withdrew from the Jacksonville Open and headed home on I-10 with the setting sun in his eyes and three thousand miles to think. It didn't occur to him that his career as a touring pro had ended, although it had. And he didn't think his kidneys would fail. But they would.

One of his boys would have to save him.

That the sons of Rick and Joan Rhoads make a good impression is not a matter for debate. Their high-profile jobs require amiability, intelligence, diplomacy – the entire catalog of virtues, in fact, asked of ambassadors to difficult countries. All three salute their father by working in his profession. Rick and his three sons all have a low-key, look-you-in-the-eye style and a gift for instruction. Seekers come to them to have their backswings unkinked and their minds untangled, a process similar to – and as painful as – psychotherapy.

Curtis, the oldest, is thirty-six. He's an assistant professional at the Olympic Club in San Francisco. "Lush" is not lush enough to describe Olympic, where the trees are slumbering giants and the air from the cold Pacific is thick and salty. Several of golf's most memorable U.S. Opens have been held there, giving a hacker on the grounds the feeling of tiptoeing through history. Including its par-three course, called the Cliff, Olympic has fifty-four holes, and many, many members and guests, so it's simultaneously exclusive and very busy. Curtis Rhoads helps keep order and ensures everyone enjoys it. He only wishes he gave more lessons.

He's always liked team sports more than golf. Today he looks like what he was, a second baseman, a point guard, and a soccer halfback. He had a pretty good golf game – he played a bit for USC – but at dinner he's more likely to talk about the Golden State Warriors of the NBA than to muse about the PGA Tour. His understatement and cooperativeness set the tone between and among the siblings. His father marveled at the harmony in his house; it hadn't been that way when he was a kid. "I was the youngest of three brothers, all of us very competitive," he recalls. "I tried to fight with 'em, but I lost every fight."

Curtis, the good teammate, deflects the credit. "It's a loving family," he says. "Top-notch on both sides. We don't have that one strange uncle no one wants to talk to."

Kevin, the middle child, is thirty-four. He's the teaching professional at The Country Club, in Brookline, Massachusetts. You remember The Country Club: it's that gorgeous course where Ouimet won and Arnie lost and the 1999 U.S. Ryder Cup team pulled a win out of its . . . hat. TCC is as upscale and private as its name implies. When Kevin is not instructing a Boston Brahmin or Brahminette, he's coaching the Harvard women's golf team. Like his older brother, he's unfailingly upbeat and polite. He looks a little like Bobby Kennedy, but with shorter hair and better teeth. He's the best golfer among the brothers, and the only one who thought about playing the Tour.

He'd been a so-so player in high school, but at UCLA he dedicated himself to the game. He won the golf team qualifying tournaments his freshman and sophomore years, but the coach couldn't accept that he'd beaten his scholarship players and didn't put him on the team – an injustice that still bothers Rick and Kevin doesn't mention. Kevin finally got his spot on the squad for his last two years, and was Honorable Mention All Pac-10 as a senior.

"Give me a minute," he says. "I want to say this right." On the eighteenth tee at The Country Club, he's been asked if, on the way to following in his father's footsteps, he didn't have some period of rebellion, some phase in which he put his hair in a ponytail and smoked Marlboros or cigarettes without a label. Kevin hits a solid drive, but a little left, into the succulent rough by a fairway bunker. From there he somehow gets a seven iron high enough to hold the scary final green. "I never felt any need to rebel, for one simple reason," he says, walking in the sunshine toward the big yellow clubhouse. "My dad is my hero."

Why? "It's hard to know that at any one time, because the criteria changes," Kevin Rhoads says. "What he did and where he worked impressed me. Watching him in the Crosby every year, how he knew players I'd seen on TV and they knew him . . . And when I went away and saw how other men comported themselves – that certainly didn't diminish him in my eyes.

"He taught all three of us to play golf, and he was always extremely encouraging. Father-son in golf instruction can be a rough dynamic. Even though both may be trying, very often it doesn't work.

"Dad's knowledge of the game was beyond question, but he never threw that in your face. At the same time, he didn't sugarcoat things. 'Here's what I think we should work on,' he'd say. 'Here's what I think might work.'"

Kevin's a strong player but he can't get a driver within thirty yards of his long-hitting baby brother. Ryan Rhoads, twenty-four, is as John Daly compared to the smooth, classic swings of his brothers. He works in the golf shop and on the lesson tee at Catta Verdera at Twelve Bridges, a golf course/real estate development in suburban Sacramento. "Painted in the enduring strokes of nature, the panoramic canvas and unspoiled beauty of Twelve Bridges at Catta Verdera has earned a distinguished seat among the legends," according to the website of one of its sales companies; a sentence of enduring, panoramic, unspoiled beauty.

Ryan's a little bigger than his brothers and a lot more social. He dropped out of golf while a student at Cal-Davis in order to focus on the demands of pretty girls and life in the Tappa Kegga Bru fraternity. After graduating, he worked for a while as a sales rep for a golf equipment company, then he, too, became a club pro.

Which of these men would have the honor and the pain and the danger of donating a kidney to his father?

After the rabies and kidney disease scare, Rick Rhoads had limped back to the family home in Moraga, a small city about an hour's drive northeast of San Francisco. He rested for three or four months until he felt strong enough to drive out to a local private course to ask if he might give lessons there. Sure, said the Yolo Fliers Club pro, Frank Elston. You can charge ten dollars, and four of them go to me. Although the terms seemed less than generous, Rick took the deal. He was too weak to fight, and he needed the money.

His luck turned early in '76. His availability for higher employment coincided with an opening for one of the best positions in the country, the head professional job at San Francisco Golf Club. He had fans on the selection committee, including the impressive Sandy Tatum, a former Rhodes scholar and the future president of the USGA. "I'd gone down to play in the L.A. Open, but flew right back when they said they wanted to interview me," Rick recalls. "I offered to withdraw from the tournament if they wanted me immediately. I think they liked that." And they liked Rick. He's been the pro at SFGC ever since, unusual longevity in a mercurial industry.

His health? Except for a little high blood pressure, no real problems. Most years he played the Bing Crosby National Pro-

Am – later called the AT&T – and a few PGA Chapter and Section events. He won both the Northern California Open and the Northern California PGA Match Play. He got checkups. But he had two ticking time bombs in his back, and he knew it. The creatinine levels in his blood gradually increased, an indication of worsening renal function. Rick didn't look well or feel well during a family gathering for Thanksgiving in 2004. "We knew the time had come," Kevin recalls. "We didn't talk about it very much. We just said, 'Let's see who's the best match, and we'll go.'"

When her husband's kidneys finally failed a few months later, "I was in shock," says Joan Rhoads. "I'm still in shock."

There may not be an uglier thing on God's green earth than a polycystic kidney. Healthy kidneys – the standard ration is two – are fist-sized, with a surface that is smooth and even and deep red. Blood flows ceaselessly through them via the creek of the renal artery, which is connected to the river of the abdominal aorta. Uriniferous tubes drain downhill. Dirty blood in through the artery, clean blood out through the veins. But polycystic kidney disease (PKD) makes it all go to hell. The blood is poorly washed and toxicity builds. Cysts form on the kidney surface and fill with fluid, turning the lovely hardworking kidney beans into discolored, misshapen football-shaped bladders – dense, very heavy football-shaped bladders. When surgeons removed Rick Rhoads's worthless, ruined kidneys, each weighed about eleven pounds. Normal is less than one pound each.

Three times a week a machine circulated and filtered his blood. During dialysis at the California Pacific Medical Center, Rick and Joan met people who'd been waiting for a kidney for years. They met others with no plans for a transplant, people who had resigned themselves to the diminished existence, constant, low-level sickness, and shortened life span of the long-term hemodialysis patient. But a transplant was the way to go if you could find a match, because a real organ cleans the blood about five times better than a machine.

Meanwhile, a life and death family drama played out. Each of Rick's blood relatives volunteered to donate: older brothers Ron and Roger, and younger sister Lorraine, the mother of touring professional Roger Tambellini. Because of their youth, the boys were always the best option, but a heart-wrenching variable hit the family between the eyes once again. Polycystic kidney disease is genetic; a fifty-fifty chance existed that Curtis, Kevin, and Ryan had inherited it. Most of the time, symptoms show up by about age thirty-five, as they had with Rick. This factor was almost enough to take Ryan, the youngest, out of the running immediately. But if his kidney matched the best with his dad, then what? All three sons of Rick and Joan took the tests.

"We *all* were ready to do it," says Ryan.

"As the oldest, I thought it was my responsibility," says Curtis.

Potential kidney donors take three tests: blood; human leukocyte antigens typing, more simply known as tissue matching; and crossmatch compatibility. Curtis and Ryan had blood drawn in San Francisco, as did Kevin in Boston. All three had the same or a similar type as their father. One test passed. Tissue matching broke the tie. This series of tests compared six antigens – markers – in the blood of the four Rhoads men. The more matches, the lower the likelihood the transplanted kidney would be rejected. Curtis matched three. Kevin and Ryan matched four.

Curtis was out.

And due to the nagging possibility that he was young enough to himself develop PKD, Ryan was out.

The clock ticked. The longer the recipient is on dialysis, the worse the chances for a successful transplant. In the final test, the crossmatch, blood from the potential donor and recipient is mixed to determine if antibodies in the recipient would treat a donated organ as an invader and try to kill it. The test was negative; the blood was compatible.

The donor would be Kevin.

He traveled to New York to meet his transplant coordinator and for x-rays, more lab tests, a physical.

"There was never a question in his mind that he'd do it," recalls Lisa Yuen, a Broadway actress and Kevin's fiancée. "He was just committed from the very start, and very calm about the whole thing. He's very humble, not someone who needs a lot of coddling. His parents phoned to ask how I felt about the operation, and then I heard the emotion in his mother's voice. And I thought, 'Oh wow, this really *is* a big deal.'"

A psychiatric social worker spoke with Kevin for an hour. A lot of "how would it make you feel" questions: if your father passed away despite the transplant; if you were found to have PKD yourself, and had to face it with only one kidney; if the transplant failed because your father didn't take care of himself.

"How would you feel if your father's body rejects your kidney?" the shrink asked.

"Excuse my ignorance," Kevin replied. "But if that happens, could I have my kidney back?" No, he couldn't.

A thousand different elements came together, from insurance to surgeons. A date was set—July 23, 2005. About two weeks before the transplant, Kevin had wrapped up another day of teaching at The Country Club when a thunderstorm came up. Golfers and staff stood in the pro shop to watch the crazy black sky and the samba of giant oaks and elms in the driving wind and rain. The storm paused for a moment. Kevin put up an umbrella and hustled out onto the path skirting the first fairway that led to the employee parking lot. Tall trees on either side gave the trail the appearance of a dark green tunnel. Suddenly a close bolt of lightning illuminated the scene, and thunder concussed the air. And just as suddenly Kevin felt transformed.

"It wasn't just the normal feeling of self-preservation," he says. "It was 'I can't get hit by lightning, because it's not just me anymore.' A pretty strong sensation. I told a member about it. He said, 'Now you know how it feels to be a parent.'"

Back in California, Rick by this time knew the misery of dialysis. After seven weeks of it, he'd experienced most of the common side effects: insomnia, weakness, nausea, and infernally itchy skin. But he didn't succumb to the worst symptom, depression. Trying to keep things light, he often asked Curtis and Ryan if they were ready to step in if Kevin's plane was late. It wasn't late.

Rick, Joan, and Kevin left for California Pacific Medical Center in San Francisco in the chilly middle of the night, because the transplant team always starts early—two complex operations, after all, two surgical teams, two anesthesias, two recoveries. Kevin drove his father's silver 2002 Nissan Maxima. Composure reigned in the car during the one-hour drive, until Kevin said, "Listen to this," and stuck a U2 CD in the player. He found the song he wanted, "Sometimes You Can't Make It on Your Own." Bono had written it for his dying father.

A few minutes later, Kevin sat on a hard bed in a curtained cubicle. The room was cool and brightly lit. His hospital gown didn't fit. He heard the sounds of nurses controlling a patient having a seizure on the right side of the curtains; on the other side of the thin fabric, a family conversed loudly and graphically about Uncle Frank's tumor. His mind raced. He pretended that the coming ordeal was like a difficult golf shot, requiring a golfer's cool – like a downhill putt to win a match. He remembered that the next day would be his birthday, and he played around with the idea that today would be "rebirth day" for his father.

"OK," he said to his kidney. "You've been a good kidney and you've done a good job. But now you have a higher calling. Now you're going on to something new." That part of his monologue went on for long minutes, and then they started an IV, and then they wheeled him into surgery.

You hear a lot of happy talk about the high success rate of kidney transplants, but reality is a lot scarier. As in any major surgery, infection, bleeding, and accidental damage to an adjacent structure are significant dangers. The danger is higher for the donor than for the recipient at first. Despite the amazing advances in immunosuppressant drugs, rejection still occurs. Sometimes the antirejection drugs cause it – a heartbreaking outcome for all concerned. And people die unpredictably on operating tables every day, most often from heart attacks or blood clots.

Kevin lay on his back. Two docs in white stood above him. The anesthesiologist and surgical nurses did what they do. The transplant surgeon cut three 3-inch-long incisions in the front of

Kevin's torso beneath his chest and a little to the side. They inserted a laparoscope, a fiber-optic instrument with a tiny light and camera on a thin flexible tube. The surgeons maneuvered it with a joystick, watching its progress on a monitor. After about twenty minutes, the kidney and its attached ureter—looking like a big bean with a dangling root—were ready to come out. Through a five-inch-wide cut made four inches below the navel, the surgeon reached his hand inside Kevin's body. He placed the kidney into a white plastic bowl filled with sterile ice. Surgeons from the other operating team came by to inspect the exact conformation of the organ they would be implanting. From opening to closing, the operation on Kevin had taken about three hours.

A nurse quickly but carefully carried Kevin's kidney across the hall to where Rick lay unconscious. A ten-inch-long incision had been made in his lower abdomen. No need to put the kidney back in his back; they fit nicely in front, and connect fairly easily to the femoral artery and the bladder. His operation also took about three hours.

Kevin's kidney functioned perfectly inside his father.

No one died.

Fourteen months later, friends dined with Rick, Joan, Curtis, and Ryan at Palomino, a busy, happy place on the Embarcadero with great food and wonderful service. Outside, the lights of the Golden Gate Bridge arced across the night as if lighting a party.

"A mojito," Joan says to Kate, the waitress, and her sons literally gasp. They've almost never seen their mother drink, and really, they don't see her drink now. She has a few experimental sips and then offers the rum and mint to anyone who wants to try it.

The topics discussed over pasta and fish are as distinct and wide-ranging as a game of *Jeopardy!*: golf, art, Barry Bonds, American cities and towns, and family. The diners lean in, the better to hear, because no one wants to miss a story or a laugh. A blush of good health and a grin paint Rick's face.

The Rhoads family aren't notable huggers or hand holders or "I love you" sayers. Their feeling for each other seems more profound than gesture and more durable than mere emotion. What they have is an attitude, a predisposition to think the best and to do the best for each other. They had that going in to the transplant, and they had it coming out.

"The experience didn't really change things between me and my dad, and I don't mean that in a negative way at all," Kevin said later, between lessons at The Country Club. "I always knew where I stood with him. But I have gained a real appreciation for the doctors and medical staffs who make miracles happen, and for the people who have to endure serious illness. I don't know how they do it. We were so lucky there was a way out."

As the two-year anniversary of the transplant approached, Rick found himself thinking about its meaning at odd times, such as on the drive to work or during a slow moment in his golf shop. "I think about where I'd be without my good fortune," he said. "I have a greater appreciation for life. I have a greater appreciation for everything. My relationship with Kevin? About the same. We were close before."

Time and jobs and geography have prevented Rick and Joan and the boys from teeing it up together in recent years. Usually, it takes a family vacation to make it happen, such as their seven-years-apart trips to Scotland and to Bandon Dunes in Oregon. But when Kevin and Lisa get married in San Francisco in the summer of '07, no one will be surprised if sometime between the rehearsal dinner and the church ceremony, the Rhoads family sneaks away to play.

2

DADDY CADDIE

Byung Wook and Michelle Wie

Mondays on the PGA Tour feel weird and uneasy, as if you left home with the iron *and* the oven on. Everyone's in limbo, caught between here and there and then and now. If you're a fan on the premises, you've made a mistake. Marco Dawson will sign your hat but the stars won't show for another day, maybe two. If you're a player, you're an early bird with six long days before you can catch a worm. Monday volunteers have no crowd to control, no traffic to direct, nothing interesting to say on the walkie-talkies, and their uniform shirts smell unpleasantly new. Time drips like a Popsicle in Nome—which is to say, slowly.

The first official day of the 2006 84 Lumber Classic at the Nemacolin Woodlands Resort and Spa in Farmington, Pennsylvania, had the usual air of disorientation plus a little more. First of all, it was September 11, the fifth anniversary of the terrorist attacks; Flight 93 crashed in a pasture only fifty miles away. The

above: BYONG WOOK LOOKS OVER THE SHOULDER OF HIS DAUGHTER, MICHELLE WIE.

hills and quiet valleys of western Pennsylvania accentuated the melancholy, as did the lack of people. The 84 is staged in a disarmingly remote spot an hour and a half from Pittsburgh at a high-end mishmash of a resort with a car museum over here and an airplane display over there. The golf courses, hotels, and amusements were financed by discount building-materials magnate Joe Hardy, whose bizarre fascination with John Daly manifests in a statue of the long-hitting abuser of alcohol and wives at the base of a Disneyesque waterfall by the fifth green, literally a monument to bad taste. The flesh-and-blood Daly wears an 84 Lumber patch on his shirt, and should.

This would be the last time TV cameras would linger on the delicate interplay of mist and the bronze John, however, at least for a while. The Tour and the Hardys had disagreed on several contractual elements, especially the length of the agreement, so the thing is being dropped. "Two big egos, neither with any give in them," said a man in a crisp red volunteer shirt. "Sad. After four years, the tournament's become a highlight around here."

But the heavy hearts caused by the tournament's lame-duck status were lightened a little by the presence of the wonder of the age, the marvelous Michelle Wie. Although her fellow competitors ignored her – "I didn't even know she was here," said imperious Ryder Cupper Scott Verplank late in the week – the sixteen-year-old Hawaiian girl jazzed the event for everyone else. Her image – and Daly's – graced the billboards dotted around the countryside, although it seemed absurd to even have billboards in burgs as small as Fairchance and Hopwood.

This would be the sixth time Michelle had been the only

woman in a men's professional event, but except for raising her profile in the world of sports and entertainment, she hadn't accomplished much playing against the boys, making only one cut, and that in a relatively small event on the Asian tour. So there she was on Monday, in remote Nemacolin, a stranger in a strange land. It was a cool day with alternating intervals of sunshine and clouds. Her pro-am group had the only gallery on the course. There were about thirty of us.

"Want a lift?" A man with a worn, friendly face has offered a seat in his cart. "Ed Misinay," he says. Ed's working for ShotLink, an IBM–PGA Tour data collection service – they chart the distances drives fly, the greens reached in regulation, and so on – but he has no shots to link until the event begins on Thursday. Ed's retired from Gallatin Bank in nearby Uniontown; he was a loan officer. Big Steelers fan. Everyone knows him. He's giving or getting the needle from someone on every hole.

We join the Wie gallery. Two impressively armed and uniformed policemen walk every step with Michelle, their eyes darting (presumably) behind the mirrored lenses of sunglasses, their torsos swollen and immobilized by Kevlar. "I wonder if there's undercover security, too," the passenger asks. "Three that I know of," Ed replies. We drive up to one of them. "Excuse me, sir," Ed says, keeping back a little so the man doesn't recognize him right away. "I think I just saw someone climb over the fence."

Michelle's manager hovers. He's Ross Berlin from the William Morris Agency, a Beverly Hills–headquartered company that represents actors (John Travolta, Kevin Spacey), actresses (Catherine Zeta-Jones, Kirsten Dunst), and directors (Quentin Tarantino), and no other golfer. Agent Berlin wears a black golf shirt, collarless, of silk or good polyester, with a colorful logo on the right sleeve. He taps a BlackBerry when he's not watching his client swing. He has great hair and a forbidding air. He didn't return my calls. The caddie is a hustling, new-on-the-job chap who acts as if he knows his leash is short. His predecessor, Greg Johnston, had been shocked to be dismissed a month previous after less than a year's service. It was messy. Berlin had done the firing, at a departure gate at the Manchester airport, after Michelle played poorly in the Weetabix Women's British Open. Have a nice flight!

Berlin himself would be gone from the Wie camp six weeks later. Jumped or pushed? It was hard to tell.

Two or three still photographers in multipocketed fisherman's vests snap Michelle from a new angle or a different background on every hole. Her playing companions are four middle-aged white men with big jobs and beer guts. They play from the member tees, while the slender island girl hits from the back. The five golfers have almost no interaction until they reach the green, because the amateurs scatter the ball all over Pennsylvania, while Michelle is down the middle.

"What's this gonna do?" one of the men asks Michelle on the fourth green. She crouches, frowning, then delivers a detailed description of the topography between ball and hole, angling her hand to illustrate: "It starts out left but then, in here, it's got to come back right, then at the hole, it's breaking left again . . ." The man sighs dramatically. "Too much information," he says, and everyone laughs.

Not laughing are Byung Wook and Hyun Kyong Wie, Michelle's parents. They march along with their daughter like emperor penguins in their black rain gear with little accents of white. They are an odd sight because you never see family inside the ropes of a Tour event, even during pro-am or practice rounds. Maybe they have some special dispensation? Byung Wook, the father, is a tall, handsome man with glasses. He's an academic. Michelle's mother, Hyun Kyong, is rounder, softer, much more a background person but no less comely. She sells real estate in Honolulu. The daughter they produced would resemble Frida Kahlo, if the tempestuous Mexican artist had been six foot one inches tall and plucked her eyebrows.

The rolling, walking, managing, securing, recording gallery observes the cannon shots Michelle hits with a driver and her nearly impeccable game from tee to green. We see Byung Wook crouch behind his daughter when she hits a full shot. He has an opinion on the proper aiming point on a blind shot, a point of view he shares with Michelle and her caddie, loudly, and with extravagant hand gestures. Hyun Kyong, the quiet one, carries a thermos of something or other; she pours a cup and hands it to Michelle. Father, mother, and daughter speak to each other in Korean. All three eat bananas, seemingly lots of them.

"Here's your chance," says Ed, who by now knows his passenger's mission. On the path by the sixth fairway, he's pulled up to the cart in which the Wies ride when they are not inside the ropes with Michelle.

"Dr. Wie?" I hold up some books I've pulled out of my briefcase. "Did you receive these? I sent them with a letter to your apartment."

"Oh, yes!" he replies brightly. He has a little bow mouth, like his daughter, and the same small skull on a long neck.

"Then could I walk with you for a few minutes and ask a few questions?"

"Not interested!" says Byung Wook Wie in the same cheery tone. He gestures to his driver, and off they go.

Ed is floored by the exchange. "'Not interested'? How about 'thanks for asking' or 'thanks for the books'? Jeez. How about 'we're not talkin' to the press today.' And you called him 'Doctor.' What kind of doctor?"

"Ph.D. in regional planning. He teaches transportation at the University of Hawaii."

Byung Wook Wie's "Not interested!" makes Ed recall his own unpleasant interaction with Phil Mickelson two years earlier. A day before the tournament started, he had some sort of patrol or assistance duty near the practice green. As a favor for his granddaughter, who loved the big left-hander, Ed carried a visor emblazoned with the Bearing Point logo, the technology and consulting company Phil represents. He approached the golfer and gently explained his mission, but instead of picking up the offered Sharpie and scratching out his name, Phil decided on a lecture. "He put his nose an inch from mine and says, 'I'm practicing my chipping now, and after that I'm gonna putt, and then I'm gonna play eighteen holes. If you're in the designated place for autographs after that, *then* I'll sign.'" Phil stomped off. Humiliated, Ed threw the visor on the ground. Every success Mickelson had from that point on resulted in a flurry of sarcastic e-mails and phone calls from his buddies, who referred to Phil as "your boy," as in "I see your boy won the Masters. Has he called you yet?"

"So this guy won't talk to you," Ed says. "Now what?"

"Well, Michelle has a press conference tomorrow at three. I could ask her why her father is such a pain."

"I'm thinking of a stronger word," Ed says.

Michelle Wie was born in Hawaii and is as American as a Big Mac, but her parents are from Seoul, where Mickey D's is called *Maekdonorugos.* Absent any input from her father, therefore, it's logical to examine the historical record for insight into the family.

Going back ten centuries, we find that Kublai, son of Genghis, sent one of his scores of daughters to marry the son of the leading family of the kingdom of Korya, solidifying his hold on the region while he attended to other business. Keeping it in the family was business as usual. In the reproductive and hereditary sense, the ferocious man who created the largest contiguous empire in world history was the most influential man ever. Genghis Khan's MO was to slaughter the males of conquered tribes, and then select their thirty prettiest women for his – ahem – temporary harem. By tracing his sturdy Y chromosome, geneticists estimate that 0.5 percent of the world's population has the legendary Mongol at the trunk of their family tree.

That the blood of the khans influenced Korea's national character is debatable, of course, and to even speak of national characteristics in a politically correct age is to skate on thin ice. But for centuries, Korea stayed by itself as much as it could, earning the nickname "the Hermit Kingdom." It is no polyglot like the United States, in other words, so some of its people's traits are as plain to the eye as dark eyes and dark hair. As for national character, Koreans may be the hardest-working, most gung-ho people on earth. This go-for-it enthusiasm shows up wonderfully at a place you might expect only love and calm reflection – Sunday services at Yoido Full Gospel Church. And what a church: it occupies a round building on the south side of Seoul, and resembles – inside and out – the "Superdrum," the basketball arena at the University of Texas. It seats twelve thousand, and they fill it up.

TV cameras bristled around the pulpit the morning of my visit a decade ago. "World's biggest church," said my host, Jong-shin Kim, the developer of a golf course near the demilitarized zone. "Seven hundred thousand members." (Now it's eight hundred thousand.) We foreign visitors were hustled into elevators and taken to the cheap seats near the rim of the bowl, where we sat in tiny hard pews. You could put on headphones and select a language for simultaneous translation of the sermon, delivered in a monotone in every language I checked. Standard stuff: "and the Lord said unto Ezekiel, go forth . . ." But live, in Korean, with the unaided ear, was the way to go, because it was not what the minister said but how he said it. Even for a veteran observer of shake-and-bake American evangelicals, the pastor and the congregation seemed amazingly fervent. At one point, the worshipers stood and raised both arms overhead three times while shouting something that could have been "Banzai!" but wasn't. The atmosphere felt warlike, and I felt ready to rumble.

Korea has a chip on its shoulder, and China, and especially Japan, put it there. Both its neighbors invaded time after time, century after century. Korea resisted bravely and often successfully, most famously in the late sixteenth century when the ingenious Yi Sun-shin led the counterattack against Japan. Despite being badly outnumbered, Admiral Yi prevailed, using armored "turtle boats" and superior tactics based on his knowledge of his country's coastline. Yi became a hero in Korea on the order of Eisenhower or Patton. But they could not turn back the invaders every time: the last occasion Japan overran the country, in the run-up to World War II, it forced the conquered people to pray to the Japanese emperor and the other Shinto deities. It also tricked or kidnapped virtual generations of Korean women – tens of thousands of people – and shipped them wherever Japanese soldiers were fighting. They were sex slaves, euphemistically known as comfort women. Directly or indirectly, the odious practice touched every Korean family.

Postwar, growing prosperity combined with Korea's history of subjugation to create a nation with an absolute desire to succeed and the means to do it. Korean autos, steel, and athletics became ascendant. South Korea's baseball team beat the U.S. in the World Baseball Classic in the spring of 2006. (While accomplishing nothing economically or socially, North Korea also has attitude; it exploded a nuclear bomb in October 2006.) A laser focus on women's golf led to incredible success. Of the top two dozen players on the LPGA tour, about half are South Korean. A baker's dozen, if you count Michelle Wie.

An important element of this frantic ambition is South Korea's hearty approval of the United States. When China took another run at its historic enemy after World War II, sparking the Korean War, the Americans came, but as defenders, not invaders or exploiters, earning an honored place in the national psyche, at least in the south. Korean businessmen literally run off the Korean Air jet when it lands in Chicago, so happy are they to be here. My interpreter during my long ago visit expressed a keen interest in getting out of ugly old Seoul, and, within a year or two, she did; Kyung Choi Bishop has hit it big selling real estate in Jacksonville.

In 1965 the U.S. Congress abolished the national origin system – which favored fair-haired types from Europe – spurring a significant emigration from Korea. By 2004, according to the U.S. Census, there were 848,000 Korean-born Americans. Byung Wook and Hyun Kyong Wie were two of these.

They seemed quite orderly about their lives. They settled in Hawaii. They called themselves B.J. (him) and Bo (her) because non-Asian Americans consistently mangled their names. He went to San José State, then to Penn, returning to his wife and Honolulu, where his publish-or-perish job compels him to write page-turners such as "A Diagonalization Algorithm for Solving Dynamic User Equilibrium Traffic Assignment Model," which appeared in *Asia-Pacific Journal of Operational Research.*

They had one child, and named her Michelle Song.

Did they do a *tol?* Most Korean parents throw a party for their baby on his or her first birthday, a tradition started centuries ago when infant mortality was high and achieving one year of age was a big deal. Guests bring gold rings or bracelets. The child is dressed in traditional clothing on *tol* day – Michelle would have looked like a little doll in a *hanbok* – and placed on a low table. Rice cookies of green and red might be placed here and there on the table, but the key items within crawling distance of the infant are a paintbrush, a coin, a pen, and a book. "She will be an artist!" the guests exclaim if the curious child picks up the brush. The coin means wealth; the pen, public service; the book, writing. "Yes, you could do other objects," says Soung Oem Davis, a Korean woman who married an American soldier. "You could have a golf club."

But the Wies surely didn't. The golf option presented itself much later. Michelle played soccer and softball without distinction, so, at age seven, B.J. handed his unusually tall daughter a tennis racket. Her ground strokes looked good, but when ordered to rush the net, she pitched a fit. And Dr. Wie, Ph.D., experienced a moment of clarity: his daughter didn't like to run. "After that," he recalled for a newspaper, "I threw away all the tennis balls and we concentrated on golf."

Did they ever. Dad and mom were competent recreational golfers (Hyun Kyong had won amateur tournaments back in South Korea) but they abandoned their own games for good so they could focus fully on Michelle. Somehow they found the time and the cash to fund several three-month training sessions at the David Leadbetter Golf Academy in Florida. Byung Wook estimates he spent $50,000 on his daughter's golf in 2002, $70,000 in '03, and $100,000 in '04. B.J. 'n' Bo's single-minded devotion to their only child – and Michelle's success – inevitably reminded people of Earl and Kultida Woods, for whom their only child was All. B.J. pinned Tiger posters on the walls of his daughter's bedroom, carried a picture of Tiger in his wallet, and kept Earl's super-involved style in his mind.

The level of attention the Woods and Wies gave to their only children seemed extraordinary, if not a little perverse, to rank-and-file American parents who only wanted the homework done and the house not burned down.

Filial devotion isn't unique around the world, of course, but it's a very strong concept in Korean culture. Mere obedience is not enough. Children have a duty to make their parents proud, and a good Korean parent must help them excel. To have an underperforming child is to lose face. This covenant between the generations leads to unity and conformity.

"I don't want to say which is better, Korean parents or Western, because both love their children big-time," says Kyung Choi Bishop, the mother of a seven-year-old girl. "Independence is very important in the U.S. Children grow up strong, and they leave the house at eighteen. Koreans – also Chinese and Japanese – are more focused on together. I never say '*I* am going to store.' We automatically say '*we* going to store.' And when the parent gets old, the child always takes care. No nursing home."

Soung Oem Davis expresses the same thing another way: "Korean parents are much more demanding than American parents. We'll do anything to help." Her son, Eddy, an assistant pro at Jimmy Clay Golf Course in Austin, recalls the sports part of his life during his childhood in Korea: "When it was decided that my brother Warren and I should learn to swim, my dad thought we should take lessons in the pool at the military base (Camp Humphreys, near Pyongtaek). My mom said no – she got us private lessons with a Korean Olympic swimmer, who worked us *very* hard. Same thing with tae kwon do; my mom insisted we learn off base. I was thirteen, my brother ten. It was six days a week, three hours a day, and no English spoken.

"My test for my black belt took place in this ancient arena with carvings all around. It was January – no heat, a concrete floor. I'll never forget the screaming from the parents of the boy I had to spar with. They thought I was bigger or more accomplished, so they just screamed that it was unfair the whole time.

"Golf has become the focus for a lot of Koreans in the last ten to fifteen years. All my mother's friends (she lives in Hawaii) play. Here, it's a recreational sport. With them, no. They do Pilates or work out to prepare for golf."

When Eddy and his three-year-old son get out the clubs, they *play*. Jaden does his no-look swing, and laughs at the reactions he gets. Eddy's advice is gentle and infrequent. But when *halmonie*–grandma–is involved, little Jaden does drills. It's real, purposeful practice.

The Wies formed a six-legged golf organism at Ko Olina, their home course on Oahu. A magazine writer watched as Hyun Kyong sat on the battered ground of the practice tee, a pyramid of golf balls by her side. She put a ball on a tall peg. She murmured something in Korean. Michelle wiggled, making an infinitesimal adjustment in her stance or posture. She swung. Mom teed up another ball, and another, and another . . . Behind them, Byung Wook peered through a camera on a tripod. Periodically during the hours-long drill, all three huddled around a laptop, their heads almost touching. "I've never seen a family so close," commented their friend, Linda Johnston. "It's almost like they are one person."

The other players on the tour hate them. Not so much the Korean girls, although they are insular, rarely attempt to learn English, and are often annoyingly good. No, the rank and file of touring pros despise their Korean *fathers*. "Daddy caddies," they call these men who carry their daughters' golf bags with such partisanship that other competitors–and sportsmanship–can disappear.

The problem erupted in 2003, when, with eighteen players on the LPGA tour, the commissioner felt compelled to call a Koreans-only meeting to go over the rules. There had been widespread and emotional complaints of illegal hand signals; equally illegal advice (in Korean) from the gallery; attempted intimidation of other caddies; and, in the most extreme case, a father kicking his daughter's ball from behind a tree. The daddy caddies responded that these were merely problems of cultural misunderstanding.

"I liked the girls, who were always friendly – although we didn't have much to talk about because of the language thing," recalls Jan Dowling, a veteran of the Futures Tour, the LPGA's feeder tour. "But their fathers looked at you funny. They were very intimidating. Their entire focus was on their daughters. For them to say 'good shot,' you had to hit a *really* good shot."

Obviously, neither side understands the other, and golf by itself does not provide enough common ground to bridge the gap. And the stories the American girls heard only made the Koreans more incomprehensible. Se Ri Pak – the most successful Korean woman golfer – had a father who drove her relentlessly. Mornings at five-thirty, dad had her run the fifteen flights of stairs in their apartment building in Taejon, first forward, then backward. She spent entire days at the practice range, even when it was so cold icicles formed in her hair. After Se Ri let it slip that cemeteries scared her, her father told her to get her sleeping bag. He drove her to the graveyard and made her spend a night alone with the dead. Another daddy caddie, this one belonging to Ju-Yun Kim – AKA Birdie Kim – was wary of unwholesome American food, so he cooked native dishes in their hotel rooms. Once the aroma of his mackerel stew so overpowered the other guests that they were asked to leave. After she won the 2005 U.S. Women's Open, Birdie, one of eleven LPGA players with the surname Kim, commented that she's "given up on being a woman," that she never wears makeup, that she thinks about golf twenty-four hours a day. When she returns home, she said, she stays at a friend's house, not with her parents, because the friend lives close to a course where she can spend all day practicing.

But Michelle has never been a puppet with her father pulling the strings, according to Bill Kwon. Kwon, a Honolulu newspaper veteran, has been writing about Michelle since she was ten. "I never thought there was a Svengali kind of thing, like Ronnie Knox or Todd Marinovich (football players with disastrously overinvolved fathers). And I wouldn't overlook the influence of Bo. There's more to her than people think, and matriarchs are very strong in Korean families.

"Even at ten, when I first heard of her, Michelle could out-hit any woman in Hawaii. She had different thoughts [about her future in the game]. I think it's fine that she plays against the men, as long as she doesn't get discouraged, and I don't think she is. Remember, she doesn't get all that endorsement money for beating girls."

Does she love the game and the circus around her playing of it, or is it all business for Michelle and the Wies? Both. "I'm happy out of my mind," the tall girl said once. "I like beating a lot of people."

Byung Wook took his turn as a daddy caddie, and endured some rough spots. His interminable putt reading at an LPGA event in 2002 resulted in a two-shot slow-play penalty; Michelle missed the cut by two. At the 2003 U.S. Women's Open – two months before that Koreans-only meeting to review on-course comportment – a fellow competitor exploded at Team Wie's rudeness. Instead of waiting for her playing partners to hit their second shots on par fours and fives, the Wies distracted the other golfers by walking quickly and directly to Michelle's drive, which was always the longest one in her group. According to witnesses, Danielle Ammaccapane screeched – their verb, not mine – at Michelle for twenty minutes afterward. The press found out about it, and Byung Wook fired himself for the final round.

Michelle missed him. "I didn't have anyone to yell at," she told writers. "It's like, 'I can't breathe! I've got to yell at someone!' I felt like I was going to explode." Those who had seen their on-course disagreements as conflict had obviously misinterpreted; the father and the daughter are devoted to each other on the course and off it.

Without a bag on his shoulder, Dr. Wie continued as a figurative daddy caddie. His enthusiasm for his daughter boiled over from time to time, compelling him to occasionally run and yell from the gallery more than is kosher. When his almost sixteen-year-old daughter turned pro, he was quite naturally involved in decisions regarding her representation and endorsements. "He's in over his head," says Wall Street veteran and consumer marketing guru William Earley of Philadelphia. "This business of playing against the men, and saying she wants to make the Ryder Cup team, and then playing poorly, amounts to muffing a product launch. Sure, she's making a lot of endorsement money, but she's also creating a large pool of doubters who may never be convinced to buy Michelle."

Michelle's three biggest deals are with Nike—which pays $5 million a year—Sony, and Omega, the watch manufacturer. Off-the-record comments from one of the three are not favorable to Byung Wook. He's made them so angry, in fact, that his behavior will be addressed in the next contract. He is, they say, the most meddlesome, difficult parent they've ever dealt with.

Early on a cool, cloudy Tuesday morning at Nemacolin, Michelle tees off by herself for a practice round. Not that she's a solitary figure—she has her parents and her caddie nearby, and, again, the only gallery—but she's awkwardly sandwiched between a twosome (in front) and a threesome behind. And although it's not a scandal or that unusual to play a practice round alone, this is Michelle Wie we're talking about. You'd think the guys might be curious. They're not. And they don't want her entourage. No one invites her to play along.

"She was gone by the time we got to the first tee," says David McKenzie, an Australian pro, part of the threesome behind. "But I wouldn't mind if she'd play a little faster." And it's true; the Wie onesome frequently holds up the following group. "Daisuke (Maruyama) said hello to her in Japanese before we teed off," says Mark Wilson, half of the twosome in front. "So it would have been on him to ask her to join us . . . But no, we don't resent her presence at all."

Byung Wook and Hyun Kyong hover like bears protecting their cub from . . . something. Just for the hell of it, when he's on the civilian side of the ropes or sitting in a grandstand, I attempt conversation with this man who doesn't want to talk to me. His enthusiasm for this game declines quickly:

"Beautiful day today."

"Very good, very good!" And:

"Michelle's playing beautifully."

"Getting better, getting better." And:

"That green's as hard as a rock. Do you think they ever water it?"

"Hmm."

On the eleventh hole, trouble. Perhaps someone has complained; maybe the tournament administration has finally noticed the ongoing breach of protocol. At any rate, it falls to the PGA Tour's player relations manager, Jimmy Gabrielsen, to drive up in a cart to inform Dr. and Mrs. Wie that, in accordance with the Tour's rules, only caddies and instructors are allowed inside the ropes. Neither can pretend to be Michelle's teacher – everyone knows they've got David Leadbetter. But Dr. Wie doesn't react well to the news. He gestures, mostly with the right hand, in a chopping motion. He raises his voice.

"We treat *you* with respect," he says. "You treat *us* with respect." Then he declaims about how he and his wife were allowed inside the ropes at the Sony Open in Honolulu, the PGA Tour event Michelle played back in January 2006.

They should give Gabrielsen the phone at the next hostage crisis. "I don't know," he says, calmly, soothingly. "I wasn't at the Sony." The Tour official remains seated in his cart, apparently not wanting the more confrontational body language implied by standing. Dr. Wie towers above him, stabbing the air like an orator building his speech to a crescendo. This doesn't look like it's going to end well . . .

A few hours later, Michelle meets the press. Five TV and

seven still photographers stand to record the proceedings, while about thirty-five seated writers take notes and ask questions. Byung Wook and Hyun Kyong sit in the back of the room. Standing near the cameramen are Michelle's instructor, Leadbetter, her peeps from William Morris and Nike, and some others not immediately identified. They watch, rapt.

Michelle performs magnificently. She utters not a single "um" or "ah" and requires no long pauses to gather her thoughts. She doesn't fidget. Hair, nails, and makeup are flawless. Only two Nike logos are visible on her person, a tasteful understatement in this ad age. The way she says the word "important" – she hits both *t*'s – is the crisp, correct pronunciation of someone who speaks other languages. In directness, honesty, and appeal, she's better at this than Tiger Woods on his best day.

"I was a loner out there today, but I got a lot of work done."

"My being here is a bigger deal for everyone else. But it's not the easiest thing in the world for a sixteen-year-old girl." (She turned seventeen on October 11.)

"Stanford." (She intends to go to college after graduating from high school, probably at the school Woods attended for a little over a year but claims as his alma mater.)

"God gave me a special talent, and I intend to use it." This is the key phrase in her response to the question about what the heck she was doing here. Her poor-to-miserable finishes against the boys in '06 had prompted negative comments from every pundit with a pen or a microphone. "It was not enlightening to see Michelle Wie, the seventeen-year-old [*sic*] American prodigy, come plumb last in a men's event in Crans-sur-Sierre, Switzerland, in September," wrote John Hopkins of the *Times* of

London. "She was being used by commercial barons for their gain, not hers."

And although she'd be last again at the 84 Lumber on Friday evening, perhaps competing at this highest level will eventually improve her as a competitor and a strategist. No one knows for sure, despite the certainty in the voices of the experts. Just as no one outside the family can say which commercial baron or parent pulls the strongest string.

Only one question throws her off: someone wants to know if she'll be a sophomore or a junior when she returns to Punahou School next week. "*Soph*omore?" she says, incredulous. "I'll be a *senior. Soph*omore. Jeez."

Her control and poise in the pressroom echo her handling of that situation in the eleventh fairway. Michelle had walked back from the green to find out what her father and the Tour manager were disagreeing about. "OK," she said after a minute, her tone all business. "My dad will stay outside the ropes. My mom will walk inside, but off to the side, not down the middle of the fairway. At least for today."

And that's what they did. If Byung Wook Wie felt chastened, he didn't show it. He's just there to support his daughter.

3

$227.05

Ben Hogan and Marvin Leonard

The man emerged from his car with the caution of a turtle poking its head out of its shell. Making his wary way across the dirt parking lot, he peered through the round lenses of his spectacles, the dim dawn light reflecting softly off his bald hatless head. He looked spindly, as if he'd been sick as a child – he had – and he didn't look that well now. He wasn't. Marvin Leonard was thirty-two in 1927 but he appeared to be a lot older.

He progressed slowly on an uphill path to the modest white-painted frame clubhouse of Glen Garden, Fort Worth's most affordable country club. This would be his second attempt at golf. He'd tried it five years earlier. Didn't like it. "I found out it took about four hours to get around this course," he recalled years later. "I thought that was silly. How could anyone stay away from work that long?"

above: Fort Worth hometown boy Ben Hogan accepts the Colonial National Invitational Leonard Trophy from the Colonial's founder, Marvin Leonard, 1952.

After the brief flirtation with the slow game, he had resumed his twelve-hour days at Leonards, the extraordinary retail conglomerate he'd started with $800 in 1918. He lived with his older sister, Enola, which sounds tame (or lame), but Marvin Leonard led a lively life away from home and the store. He attended Cats minor league baseball games and meetings of Lions, Salesmanship, Rotary, Kiwanis, and Ku Klux Klan Number 101 – he joined everything. He went to nightclubs or to the movies with eligible ladies who liked his East Texas accent or his money. He drank. Eventually, the pace caught up with him. His fatigue was so profound, his stomach so sour, that he felt compelled to consult his physician, who told him to "start playing golf or start preparing for a crackup." But the lure of commerce never lifted. When he went to buy a set of hickories at Trav Daniels Sporting Goods Company, Marvin took the opportunity to hire away the enthusiastic young man who waited on him, because his store needed a new manager for hard goods. Now that he had golf clubs, Marvin took a break.

Thus, Glen Garden at sunrise. But could even the world's most absorbing game relieve the stress from sadness and success that accumulated in this one year? 1927 had been a killer, and it wasn't over yet. Business was booming – Leonards was on its way to its first year of $1 million in sales – but achieving this height had required some big gambles. After years of occasional spending on newspaper ads, Marvin and his partner and younger brother Obie committed to a big weekly splash of ink in the *Star-Telegram.* A new sandwich counter and soda fountain represented another risky addition to overhead, because who ever heard of eating in the same building where you bought your cottonseed and your tractor parts? In the planning stage for December was a third expensive experiment: Toyland, effectively a Christmas theme park, the centerpiece of the largest, most spectacular toy department in town. They'd launch the thing with fireworks, and Santa would broadcast from the store on KGKO every afternoon at four o'clock from Thanksgiving through Christmas.

These projects added to Marvin's baseline worry about avoiding debt and keeping the labor unions the hell away from his employees. And his father's death in June added a shadowy element to his lack of ease. Although the conservative part of his personality—and the idea of going into retail in the first place—had come from Obadiah John Thomas Leonard, the patriarch and his ninth child had not been close. A bearded, humorless man, Obadiah glared at the camera for a family portrait in 1901, and his wife Tiny and the seven surviving children (out of ten births) likewise stared unflinchingly at posterity. Obadiah, born in Georgia, and Tiny, in Alabama, were part of the big westward migration after the Civil War. Their children's names—among them Green, Cora Suvelia, and Byrdie Clementine—were as country as grits.

The Leonards lived in little Linden, in northeast Texas, near the borders with Arkansas and Louisiana. They weren't poor, exactly, but they were *very* frugal. Father, who ruled the roost like the Old Testament God, demanded silence during a Bible reading between the morning and evening Sunday church services. "Thou shalt beat him with the rod, and shalt deliver his soul from hell"; at least half a dozen proverbs justified his belief in vigorous corporal punishment for misbehaving children. "Papa was pretty hard," understated Enola. And he treated debt like an eighth deadly sin. During the approximately four years he owned and operated John Leonard, Dealer in General Merchandise, he borrowed no money to stock his store, and blamed its failure on those who owed him but failed to pay in a timely way. He went back to farming. Marvin, frail from two bouts with pneumonia, hated farming. He particularly despised the sweaty effort of plowing, when clods of dirt and roots ricocheted off his thin shins, and the swaying back-end of a donkey mocked his ambition and view of the future. Struggling to work the land didn't endear to him the daddy who made him do it.

As an adult, Marvin made it clear that he loved his mother but about his father he had little to say. Obadiah's name came up only when Marvin told one of the half-dozen stories he pulled out of his pocket to emphasize – no matter how rich and important he'd become – that he was still just a country boy at heart, doin' his best in the big city. There was The Night He Refused to Eat the Spinach he was served for dinner, and got the same spinach for breakfast the next morning; and The Pants That Were So Patched they were more patch than pants. A Suit Too Dear told why he didn't get a diploma from Linden High School: he didn't want to burden the family with the expense of buying him new clothes for the graduation ceremony. And The Lost and Found Fortune: one day when he was a kid, Marvin dropped a nickel on the porch and it rolled between the floorboards. The child searched for a while and was ready to declare the coin lost, but Obadiah made him look – "all day" according to the way Marvin told the story – until it was found.

When little Marvin finally found his nickel, he received no congratulations. You shouldn't have lost it in the first place, his father declared.

Mr. Leonard always had an audience when he pulled into the dirt lot at Glen Garden. Even at this hour a couple of boys would have been standing like prisoners behind an adjacent fence, observing the Cadillac's frog's-eye headlights and its mile-long hood. The kaleidoscope of glare on its windshield obscured the identity of the driver but the caddies knew who he was. Someone would have delivered the ritual scouting report: *That's Leonard. Nice guy, lousy golfer, nickel tip. You know, "More Merchandise for Less Money"—that Leonard. Your loop, Benny.*

Most of the days of his adolescence—increasingly, even school days—fifteen-year-old Benny waited for a job in the wooden pen. Other kids on the clueless cusp of manhood loitered with him, compensating for their uncertainty by acting as caricatures of men. They were anonymous occupants of the bottom rung of the social and economic ladder, none of them older than sixteen, all of them anxious to earn 65 cents. They rolled dice and smoked cigarettes while waiting for work, and the F-bombs or *goddamns* they dropped like daredevils into every sentence stiffened their resolve. They fought each other with fists and acted cruelly to newcomers. Benny embraced this cold-blooded worldview, which taught a boy to serve but never to surrender.

Skinny Benny was Mr. Leonard's caddie because he was always there and because he was the best, or almost the best, golfer in the caddie yard. In theory, at least, he might help a new player. Marvin Leonard liked to have Benny on his bag because he was a student of humanity. The buttoned-up boy fascinated Marvin; he seemed so old for fifteen. The usual caddie-golfer relationship involved brief, polite comments from the employee—"good shot, sir!"—and as much monologue as the employer cared to put forth. But neither of these two was typical: the man was as expert at prying out confessions as the best psychologist, while the boy was as likely to bare his soul as he was to levitate.

So they walked along between the hours of seven and nine A.M. in the late summer of '27. Later in the day, with the unbroken beige of its sand greens and its unwatered fairways shimmering in the heat, Glen Garden would resemble a golf hellscape but the cooler morning light and air softened its look somewhat. Mr. Leonard—or Mr. Marvin, as his thousands of customers called him—pecked rather gingerly at the ball, a rubbery, low-miles-per-hour stroke he would never lose. Between swings, he would have asked his caddie personal questions because that was his habit with everyone. Marvin always spoke very slowly:

You have any brothers, son?

Yes, sir. One. Royal.

Any sisters?

Yes, sir. One. Princess.

Interesting names. Tell me about your parents, Ben.

I got a mom. Dad's dead.

Dad's dead. But Benny's father was more than just dead. His suicide five years earlier had so shocked the editor of the *Fort Worth Record* that he'd placed the story in the center of the front page. The shock wasn't so much that a man with a history of mental illness in a shotgun shack in a lousy neighborhood had pressed a .38 revolver to his chest and pulled the trigger—no, the really horrifying, titillating part of the drama involved nine-year-old Benny. He'd apparently been sitting there when it happened. He heard the gunshot, smelled the smoke, saw the blood. And got a headline: CHILD OF 6 SEES HIS FATHER SHOT. Benny was actually nine years old, but he was small for his age, and looked younger.

This was his closely guarded secret and the untreated psychic wound he hid all his life.

And all his life he remembered his father every time he looked in a mirror. He looked identical to Chester facially, and was built the same – long, strong monkey arms on a taut but average-sized torso. In happier times, Chester had taken his sons to work with him, cementing the father-son bond in a way that was typical early in the last century but not much seen anymore. Chester was a blacksmith, and the son of a Mississippi-born blacksmith. His mother was from Alabama. "That's my boy, Ben," Chester would say; according to a customer, the proud father often introduced his kids to anyone coming in with a broken plow or an unshod pony. Maybe Royal or Ben would be smiths, too. They weren't, as it turned out, but hard work and fixing or forming things out of metal would be a part of Benny for the rest of his life, and those were profound gifts from papa. But then Chester shot a hole through everyone and everything.

The cliché would be that the boy without a father and the man without a son found what their hearts desired in each other, and that golf facilitated the deal. But the Hogan and Leonard relationship was complicated; they were tyro and tutor in some respects, and both played each role. They were also peers and business partners. They became best friends.

The golfer and the caddie trudged along on the rock-hard golf course, forging their unlikely bond.

Ben Hogan Account with J. M. Leonard
1931
when he left for California $50
12/21/31 wired for $100 which we sent 100.
12/21 charges for wiring 100. 2.05
1/9/32 sent check to him in California 75.
TOTAL 227.05
Ben Hogan also owes us $15. on an old Athletic Equipment Company account.
2/2/32 BH was in the office and talked with JML

Sunrise golf had a good effect on the fragile constitution of Marvin Leonard. He'd return to his apartment and to his sister Enola with, for a change, an appetite. "It wasn't long until I was eating a good breakfast – eggs, oatmeal, bacon," he recalled. Tuesday, Thursday, and Sunday golf games became a ritual, and he joined upmarket River Crest Country Club while retaining his membership at Glen Garden, and his contact with that intriguing caddie.

Step by step, Marvin fell deeply in love with the game. He advanced from those solitary walks with Bennie to foursome golf and its attendant camaraderie, low-stakes gambling, and postround drinking. Marvin took his game on the road – to California, in particular – and played other, better golf courses. His take-charge personality would not allow him to merely play golf, however; he had to improve it. Soon after accepting a seat on

Glen Garden's Board of Directors, he convinced the club to tear out the bumpy but heat-loving Bermuda grass on the eighteenth green and replace it with immeasurably smoother but heat-shunning bent grass, the surface he'd enjoyed so much on various courses up north. No one had tried this before in the Southwest – but with copious watering the experiment worked, and it made Marvin think about the possibilities.

Meanwhile, his golf technique and results improved. To compensate for his rather gentle swing, he hooked every shot, because hooks hit the ground and roll. Although he never hit the ball very far or particularly solidly, he holed a lot of putts with a blade putter and a loosey-goosey stroke. His scores crept down into the 80s. As Benny observed this metamorphosis in the year they met regularly, and their friendship slowly grew, he found that there was something he desperately wanted to say to Mr. Leonard. But he dared not say it.

Opportunities for the poor boy to say anything to the rich man soon dried up, however. Benny turned sixteen in August 1928 – too old, according to the club's rule, to carry clubs at Glen Garden. He asked if he might at least be allowed to continue to hit balls on the practice fairway the caddies used when no members were around. The club manager said no. So in his sixteenth year Benny dropped out of Paschal High – he wasn't attending much anyway – and shifted his base of operations to Z Boaz, Katy Lake, and Worth Hills, Fort Worth's modest daily-fee courses. He was a player now, not a mere caddie. Obsessive practice made him good; an attitude so competitive it blotted out the sun made him *very* good. Going by Ben, not the diminutive Benny, he finished second in two big amateur tournaments and turned pro before his eighteenth birthday. He did not desire to be a club professional, and didn't have the personality for it, anyway; he wanted only to prove himself in tournaments. He hit the label off the ball, but too often his long, ferocious swing with a driver sent his ball into the shade. Success would mean he'd become *somebody,* not just another victim of circumstances. If he failed, he wouldn't be much worse off. But he was broke, and getting broker.

The angels sang when Ben allowed himself to be helped by the very rich, very kind man he had caddied for a couple of years before. Marvin would have gone to him, intimates of both agree—not vice versa. Chester Hogan's suicide had created a detached, distrustful young man, so the loan must be regarded as a milestone. In the long run, the symbolism of the transaction was more important than the entry fees and tanks of gas it bought.

For their meeting in February 1932, the nineteen-year-old golf pro would have had to walk past the pianos and refrigerators in the Furnishings department to get to Marvin's modest office on the second floor.

Other people in need walked the same path—Ben wasn't the only one getting Marvin's cash. "My father liked young people and enjoyed being a mentor," recalls his daughter, Marty Leonard. "Waiters, our paper boy—just anyone who needed encouragement, a role model, and some money. My dad was so tuned in. I'm still hearing new stories about people he helped.

"I think he just saw the potential in Ben."

The Leonard brothers could afford philanthropy because they were printing money—literally. In desperation as the world-wide economic crisis peaked in March 1933, President Roosevelt ordered the closing of every bank in the United States. Marvin and brother Obie responded ingeniously, by producing their own paper dollars in denominations of one, five, and ten. Worker bees cashed their paychecks and got Leonard's scrip in return; amazingly, merchants all over town accepted the party-colored rectangles as real currency. Standing in for the banks made the Leonard boys heroes in Fort Worth, and their giving amplified their status. During those interminable years of the Depression, men with hungry children but no money would not be given credit—the Leonards didn't believe in credit—but they would be invited to fill up their carts with groceries, no charge. When a Tarrant County program to provide school lunches for poor kids ran out of funds, Marvin kept it going with a gift of $35,000. He gave Lena Pope's home for orphaned and neglected children even more than that.

In this context, Leonard's loan to Hogan wasn't very much and it wasn't unusual, either. Although $227.05 was not an insignificant sum at a time when $495 would buy a new Chevy coupe, friends and fans of both men often overstate Marvin's financial aid. Because except for that one interval, he didn't finance Hogan on the tour; after he went through that initial stake, Ben didn't accept any more help. Hogan was always the champion of doing things for himself.

He practiced and lived poor. In the years 1930 through 1936, Hogan's official winnings as a professional golfer were zero; zero; $200; $50; $112; zero; and zero. He supported himself by fixing cars and by carrying suitcases in a hotel. He took two club pro jobs that paid almost nothing. Probably his most profitable gig—

and one that embarrassed him ever after – involved dealing cards and overseeing dice throwers in various illegal but tolerated backroom games in downtown Fort Worth. The players and whores and hangers-on drank Prohibition booze, awkwardly disguised in teacups. Grim, handsome Ben shuffled and dealt and brought his money home to Valerie, the brown-haired country girl he'd married in April 1935. They saved like squirrels to buy a used Buick to travel the country for one long last shot at the tour. During a bleak spell in California, they came within an eyelash of quitting the whole business due to lack of funds, and still Hogan wouldn't borrow any more from his rich friend in Fort Worth.

Meanwhile, Marvin had become so enamored of the patch of bent grass he'd grown at Glen Garden that he tried very hard to induce River Crest to dig up its Bermuda grass surfaces and replant with the smooth northern grass. According to legend, someone suggested he build his own course if he wanted bent grass greens so damn much. So he did.

Colonial Country Club opened in January 1936. Hogan was around from the start, practicing so much he practically lived there. With its superb design and overall air of luxury and money, Colonial was a huge improvement for the impoverished pro over Z Boaz. There's no record of him paying any dues, indirect evidence of more largesse from the club president and sole owner. There were stretches when Ben and Marvin saw each other daily, sometimes, hourly.

How close did they become? How did they think of each other? Marvin fathered four children in the 1930s – all daughters – named Mary, Miranda, Martha ("Marty"), and Madelon – so the role of Marvin's son appears to have gone unfilled. But it wasn't, at least not in the sports sense. "I was a tomboy," recalls Marty, "and the only girl on the elementary school football team." Marvin didn't want the other kids to take it easy on his daughter just because of her gender. "Hit her!" he shouted from the sidelines during a game. "Hit her hard!"

Marty got good at golf, and her father accompanied her to tournaments. During their lengthy summer vacations, the entire family encamped near the excellent courses (and bent grass greens) at The Broadmoor in Colorado, in Santa Barbara (they played at Montecito Country Club), and on the Monterey Peninsula. Marty remembers the time they spent two and half months at The Lodge at Pebble Beach. Hogan visited.

Correlation isn't causation—I flap my arms and no elephants appear in my yard, but the elephants don't stay away *because* I flap my arms—but a lot of Hogan's style and attitude seems to have come from Leonard. Cars, for example: Marvin drove Cadillacs, Ben drove Cadillacs (as soon as he could afford one). Clothes: conservative and impeccable for both, and suits and ties whenever possible. Politics: right of right center (although he was tolerant, even enlightened on matters of race, Leonard stayed with the KKK for a number of years because of its anti-union, anti-Bolshevik dogma; in an interview in 1970, Hogan expressed his disappointment in the Nineteenth Amendment to the Constitution, which gave women the right to vote). Both feared flying.

At table, Marvin preferred only the best. Kansas City beef and Denver lamb graced his plate; Hogan became similarly fastidious about food (as soon as he could afford to be). In about 1970, Ben and his wife Valerie were part of a party of eight for dinner at a private club in Houston called Maxim's. "The maitre d' comes out and says, 'What can I prepare for you this evening?'" recalls Jimmy Stroope, an oilman and an excellent amateur golfer who teed it up with Hogan a few times. "And Ben says 'I think I would like veal piccata.' And then he goes into the kitchen to watch them or help them make it. We all ate veal piccata that night."

As for other elements of the good life, both Leonard and Hogan smoked like coal furnaces; for a while, Ben copied Marvin's use of a cigarette holder. Although the young Hogan wasn't much of a drinker, Marvin was. A do-as-I-say supporter of Prohibition, Leonard filled his wine cellar with whiskey – two staples were Old Worthy scotch and Old Fitzgerald bourbon. He had a long martini stage – Hogan shared it. Marvin had a couple every day, and usually a couple more, but he rarely wobbled or slurred. In later years, when Ben kept up with his friend in the nineteenth hole, they drank the same stuff in the same impressive volume and still maintained their dignity.

There was a lot about Marvin that Ben simply couldn't emulate, such as his ease with and curiosity about strangers. But in the absence of Ben's father, Marvin Leonard provided one very good example of how to interact with the world.

Yet despite all their time together, and their unmistakable pride in each other's accomplishments, there remained that one thing Ben wanted to say to Marvin, but couldn't. Not yet.

After all his tournaments were won, and his equipment company had been started, had succeeded, and then had been sold, Ben Hogan lived a very steady life. He never said so, but the highlight of his day must have been lunch. After a two-hour appearance at his office, and still in his conservative business suit with his tie still tightly knotted, he sat – always in the same chair – at a round table by a window on the second-floor Men's Grill at Shady Oaks Country Club. He had a great view of the ninth and eighteenth greens and at the green grass and live oak trees beyond. Light reflected off the large lenses of his spectacles. Decades passed. There was something machine-like in the way the old gentleman drew his left hand to his lips, and then his right, the first holding a cigarette, the second, a drink. He looked stoic, not nostalgic, but you wonder if he ever thought about his old friend during these moments.

Hogan knew that the first occupant of his chair by the window had been Marvin Leonard. After Leonard had sold Colonial to its members and realizing that Fort Worth needed another place to play and that he needed another big project, he built his second golf course. During construction of the Shady Oaks clubhouse in 1957 and 1958, Leonard took pains to ensure a pleasing vista for future diners, so when the foundation for the Grill was dug too deep, he had it filled in. Every day, while table saws whirred and sawdust filled the air, he pulled up a chair and sat by the window, the window that would one day be Hogan's.

If Ben thought about Marvin in that dreamy hour after lunch, he might recall the five times he won the PGA Tour event his friend had started on the course he'd founded (both called Colonial). He couldn't get one golf disappointment out of his mind, and Marvin had been part of that, too: in 1960, at age forty-seven, Ben had made one last desperate attempt to win the U.S.

Open. But a perfectly struck wedge shot on the second-to-last hole had spun off the seventeenth green at Cherry Hills and into the water, costing him a bogey, and, probably, the tournament. On the long train ride back home from Denver, Ben talked very solemnly and at length about his profound disappointment. The only passengers in their club car were Ben, Valerie, Gene Smyers, a well-met insurance man from Fort Worth, Marvin, and his daughter Marty.

As he gazed out the window, and smoked, and drank, Hogan might also have recalled the fortune he'd made with Marvin drilling oil and gas wells in Comanche County. Before that, when Hogan had no real money and his nascent golf equipment company was on the ropes financially, his dear friend had come through with a loan that was every bit as welcome as the one that got him on the tour in 1931. It was interesting to observe the way Ben dropped his guard and ran his business like Marvin ran his. He knew everyone's job and everyone's name and his office door was usually open, especially for the boys in sales. Each employee was part of the family – but if any family member decided to join a union, he was welcome to draw his wages and get the hell off the property. Ben hated the idea of organized workers, same as Marvin.

Thanks to his mentor, Hogan extended his greatest asset on the golf course – his unshakable belief in himself – into the business world. How's this for confidence: Jimmy Stroope recalls inviting Hogan to his office in Houston to discuss oil investments. "I showed Ben several drilling prospects we were working on and explained the [payment] formula I used for investors, which, incidentally, were some of the most prominent and wealthy in Houston. When I finished, he said he wanted a quarter of my deals at no cost because I would be using his name. I thought he was kidding. When I realized he wasn't, I explained I did not need him as my investor base exceeded my needs. We never discussed business again."

If Hogan fell into reverie those afternoons and thought about Marvin, he probably did not dwell on the time he got to thank him publicly for his friendship and benevolence.

Ben had been the keynote speaker at the Marvin Leonard Appreciation Dinner at Colonial in April 1968, and it was said that he prepared for his speech as if he were getting ready for the U.S. Open. He decided to try for a humorous tone. Big mistake: although one report referred to the "side-splitting laughter" his remarks produced, film of the event reveals that few sides were split. "We here in Fort Worth like to honor people who have never made a success of anything," he said with leaden sarcasm. "We only honor complete parasites." The audience tittered uneasily. Ben could hit a high one iron off a downhill lie but he couldn't do funny.

His talk improved when he dropped the bullshit. Hogan recalled that when he finally made some money as a professional golfer, he tried to repay the money that got him started. Marvin refused. "I just wanted you to ask," Ben said he said.

Marvin looked like hell that night and didn't react to the good speeches or the bad. He was already ill from the cirrhosis that would take his life two years later. When he died, did Hogan mourn for his second father?

One test of the closeness of their bond would be if Ben *told* Marvin.

Psychologists say that children who survive a parent's sudden death can come to grips with it if they have a support system, someone with whom to talk about their loss. But, until the end of his life, when he told all to his private nurse, Hogan didn't talk about his father's suicide. Apparently even Valerie was in the dark about this until they'd been married a number of years. Byron Nelson grew up with Ben and competed with him over the decades but he didn't learn of the suicide until he read about it in a book called *The Eternal Summer* in 1993. There's zero indication that Marvin knew. None of the friends or family of both thinks he knew.

Was Ben a surrogate son? Did Marvin become the father Ben lost so inexplicably? No, probably not, says Marty Leonard: they were peers and great friends, she says, not a son and his dad.

No, says Gene Smyers, a member at Colonial and Shady Oaks who was close to both Hogan and Leonard: "Marvin liked and admired Ben. Ben loved Marvin – and dogs. But Ben never *ever* talked about his own father."

No, says Gary Laughlin, a Fort Worth oilman who knew both men intimately: "Ben Hogan was more or less self-made."

No, says Paul Leonard, Marvin's nephew: "Uncle Marvin was his mentor in business matters and they were very good friends . . . their lockers at Shady Oaks were side by side."

Maybe, says Dr. James Knestrick, a nationally known psychologist based in Philadelphia. "But I don't think you're looking closely enough at Chester. Hogan's father was a competent man, not a drunken slob, and Ben simply couldn't blame him for the suicide. He obviously did not blame his mother – he protected her for the rest of her life. He blamed himself. Ben thought: 'I must be really flawed.' So he demonstrated his lack of flaw for the rest of his life, in the way he treated his mother and his wife, and how he spoke and dressed – and, of course, in his golf. Carrying out his duties so responsibly was how he fought off depression."

Following an emergency appendectomy in 1992, Hogan fell into a prolonged and dangerous delirium. For over two weeks he didn't know where he was. Valerie hovered, worried to distraction. A psychiatrist called in to bring him back to consciousness observed that Hogan appeared to think he was playing golf, and at times he spoke to people long dead.

So what was the thing that Hogan waited all those years to say to Leonard? He'd finally said it one day on the Shady Oaks practice tee. After observing for the ten thousandth time Marvin's cooked noodle golf swing, Ben could stand it no more.

"Goddammit Marvin, *hit* the ball," he said. "Don't just swing at it. *Hit* it, goddammit."

Leonard smiled indulgently and tapped another shot the same old way.

4

ULSTERMEN

Billy and David Feherty

A couple of times when we were kids, my brothers and I were invited to load clubs and clothes and secret stashes of candy into our white four-door Ford Galaxie 500. Dad drove south down the sullen Ohio highways, too slowly for us. We studied the decreasing height of the dirty, crusted snow on the side of the road, waiting for it to disappear altogether as we arced across the Mason-Dixon line. Gatlinburg, Tennessee, a wondrous tourist trap in the Smoky Mountains, was only marginally warmer than the Buckeye State during spring break but it felt like the tropics to us.

Freed from the competition for food and clean socks at home, our band of brothers bonded in new ways. One of us observed at a fuel and bathroom break that you don't really take a pee, you leave one. Hilarious! Many more laughs ensued as we ridiculed our favorite underclass, hillbillies. What are the three Rs for a hillbilly? Readin', ritin', and Route 77. What's the capital of West Virginia? Akron. To explain our clever brand of humor: many people from West-by-God Virginia had migrated to our vicinity to work at jobs in the car and car tar – car *tire!* – industries. They made a handy target.

I suppose my father was happy we were having fun. Now that time has changed my role from passenger on golf trips to guide, I monitor my sons' enjoyment levels like a nurse checking temperatures. So it was a year ago, when I took my youngest on our biggest trip ever, to Ireland. But we both felt pressure, and while I knew we'd have an adventure, I wasn't sure there'd be any fun. John's mother, my ex-wife, had chilled the atmosphere by declaring her lack of support or cooperation and her opposition to John missing five days of ninth grade. I added the weight of her leaden negativity to the pile of rocks already on my back. My father had just died.

We went. We stayed in the north of the Republic of Ireland and in Northern Ireland and played golf by the sea. I loved the Mussenden Links at Castlerock and would have gone a second eighteen but for my fellow traveler's fatigue. We drove to the Inishowen Peninsula and played wild, sublime Ballyliffin, a course for the gods. The soft green hills and very cool wet weather off the North Sea wore John down, so I carried his clubs. He didn't play at all the second nine, and he trudged along twenty yards behind me, a beanpole fourteen-year-old in jeans and three jackets, alone with his thoughts.

We stopped in Buncrana on the way back, and tried the course by the side of the road, the North West Golf Club. Loved it, and loved the welcome mat put out by the pro, Seamus McBriarty.

Postround, we sat on the second floor of the clubhouse and looked out over the flat course. Beyond the blue ribbon of the Lough Swilly, the Mouldy Mountains dozed. Over a beer, and through cigarette fumes, and apropos of nothing much, Seamus mentioned that David Feherty was a friend of his.

"Look right or die," John repeated ten times a day as I negotiated, more or less successfully, driving on the left round roundabouts and on side streets no wider than cart paths. We visited two cemeteries in Limavady, looking for a stone reminder of my great-great-aunt Annie Lindsay, who had given my mother beautiful wool coats, among other things. We didn't find her grave, but I put my hands on the pebbly surface of her house at 11 Irish Green Road—a dentist's office now. Who are you? I asked myself as I touched the pale stucco walls. What is most deeply you, the you with all the water burned off, like the stuff at the bottom of a coffee pot left on too long? Maybe fathers and mothers are the wrong place to look. Perhaps the momentum in life is the result of an invisible push from someone from two generations ago—or ten, or a hundred.

At the end of the week we relaxed in the super-cool Ten Square Luxury Hotel in downtown Belfast. We were weary, slightly golfed-out, and possibly a little homesick, but Irish hospitality had made it a wonderful trip. I made plans to have a pint or two at the Belfast Telegraph, where Bono and Colin Farrell go for a Guinness when they're in town. The Belfast Visitor and Convention Bureau called to confirm our meeting on Monday morning, a conference that would turn out to be a bit awkward. Everything was beautiful. Then everything went to hell.

Shortly before we arrived, stocky white men wearing black

ties and white shirts draped with orange sashes staged their annual Whiterock parade in West Belfast, the purpose of which, according to their website, was "an expression of Orange culture." (Orange means Protestant.) The Garda – police – were on hand because the parade had a history of violence; to forestall more trouble, they ordered a one-hundred-meter detour to avoid a fervently Catholic segment of Springfield Road. To hell with that, said the men of the Orange Order. These streets belong to us as much as to those Fenian bastards. They shoved, they shouted, and a couple of them gestured menacingly with their ceremonial swords. The group wearing red faces with orange accents threw bricks and the ones dressed like Darth Vader deflected them with plastic shields; the two sides seemed made for each other. The odd violent dance continued that night, when Orangemen or Orange sympathizers set cars on fire. When Gardaí and firemen came out to investigate and extinguish, angry young men opened up with petrol bombs, paint pellets, and automatic weapons. It was on TV. Nighttime helicopter shots showed streaks of fire arcing slowly down from rooftops to the street.

The most shocking incident in a weekend filled with them was the bus hijacking in Bangor, a coastal city thirteen miles east of Belfast. A couple of – thugs? terrorists? zealots? – stole the motor coach, drove it away from its route, robbed the passengers, kicked them out at Saint Andrews Church after a fifteen-minute ride, parked the bus so as to block Green Road, and "set it alight," to borrow a frequently used phrase from the *Belfast Telegraph.* The hijackers then pitched gasoline grenades at the firemen when they arrived.

As we walked to a movie theater near the Ten Square, John

and I followed a smoke cloud and the smell of burning rubber to a smoldering car. We marveled at the scars from pipe bombs and paint guns on the olive drab, wedge-shaped assault vehicle parked at the scene, an intersection of roads whose names I can't recall. Three or four officers with restless eyes talked on radios and appeared annoyed at us for looking at them and the car like it was a tourist attraction.

The worst religious conflict in Belfast in ten years had required the presence of one thousand policemen and one thousand soldiers. The BBC reported that fifty Gardaí were hurt. Arrests and civilian injuries ran into the hundreds but apparently – amazingly – no one died. Despite its fury, this spasm hadn't been deadly violence so much as a reminder of it.

The bombs and riots were more common and more deadly when David Feherty was a wee boyo.

He grew up in Bangor, Northern Ireland, the city shamed in September '05 by that bus hijacking. The Fehertys – William and Vi and their children Helen, David, and Deborah – were Church of Ireland and thus part of the uneasy 55 percent Protestant majority – uneasy because the rest of Eire is overwhelmingly Catholic. If a hand placed flat on a table represents the entire island, Northern Ireland is the top half of the three middle fingers. It's about a sixth of the land mass and has a quarter to a third of the population.

Northern Ireland is part of the United Kingdom and its residents are British citizens. English troops stand by in case of trouble. Some are soothed by their presence and others, to put it mildly, resent it.

Histories of the top of the three fingers can confuse, because Irish historians grind axes as much as any, and they have so many axes to grind. And the euphemisms and labels you encounter can make you forget who is fighting whom, so it's handy to prepare a simplified lineup card. In this corner: Protestant-Orange-Unionist-Loyalist-Williamite-English Northern Ireland; and in this corner, Catholic-Green-Nationalist-Nativist-Jacobite-anti-English Republic of Ireland. Don't shake hands. Come out insulting each other. "Belfast was Baghdad with shitty weather," Feherty says, betraying his gift for one-liners. "But we played with Catholic kids all the time. We were never allowed to understand the reason for the hatred."

The hatred bloomed in 1601, when England topped Ireland in the Nine Years War and acted like it now owned the place. As English and Scottish Protestant settlers moved in, native Catholic Irish were pushed out — to poorer land, or to paying rent on what were once their own fields and farms. The dispossessed rose up in 1641 and Ulster — one of Ireland's four provinces — was the principal northern battleground. Anyone who wants to understand the country must also look at the events of 1846, which were probably enough by themselves to ensure a durable hostility. That was the year fungus turned the potato crop to inedible black slime, a disaster for a poor nation that ate spuds with every meal or for every meal. Ireland produced plenty of other crops and grains and livestock that could have averted holocaust but absentee owners refused to share and the English government would not step in. They let them die, seemed to want them to die. The phrase "surplus Irishmen" had some currency. Starving farmers were evicted and their houses torn down as they watched. Several million Irish sailed to North America and tens of thousands died of starvation.

It's tempting to recite more dates and one-sentence summaries as if in answer to "Trace the roots of the historical conflict between England and Ireland" on an undergrad history exam. A clever student might simply reproduce that oft-quoted bit of glibness from a pundit named Sidney Littlewood: "The Irish don't know what they want and are prepared to fight to the death to get it."

The big History of Ireland affected the little history of the Fehertys. William—Billy—worked the docks in Belfast for Ulster Ferry, a container freight company, estimating the damage suffered to goods coming off ships and filing the appropriate insurance claims. But The Troubles resumed in Ulster in the late 1960s. Bloody Sunday, IRA, UVA, Sinn Fein, English soldiers, Bernadette Devlin—a new cast performed the old play. The local economy went to hell. Billy Feherty lost his job. He was forty-two; his middle child was eight.

"My sisters and I didn't understand it, but he was devastated," David recalls. "There was a family talk. Dad told us he'd be starting his own business, doing the same thing, and call it Freight Fast. I tried to help by stealing some office supplies from my teacher, Mrs. Cordelia Geddes. She had this big knuckle-duster ring and she'd whack you on the head with it . . . Well, Dad marched me right back to her and made me tell her what I'd done."

Not the only bad memory of school: this man with a lightning-fast mind squirmed and daydreamed as math and science and Shakespeare and Thomas Hardy bounced off his head. His teachers thought him stupid. "I was just classic ADD," recalls

Feherty. One day, while sitting in a geography class and not listening, he decided he would quit the academic torture and begin a career as a professional golfer. It was a bold decision for a seventeen-year-old, but he'd shown tremendous promise in the game. Hadn't he?

"No. I sucked," Feherty says. "I had about a five handicap. I was probably one hundredth best in our club. I know my father endured a lot of ridicule. My Uncle Jack said to him, 'Do you have *another* son named David? Because for the one I know, turning pro . . . not a good idea.'

"I thought my father was going to be furious about my decision. But he looked at me and said, 'Does it give you goose bumps?' And I said, 'Yeah, it does.' I imagined meself winning the British Open."

And so it came to pass – the pro part, not winning the Open. Feherty kissed his family goodbye and took the long journey to the Mid-Herts Club in Hertfordshire, England, to begin his apprenticeship. Half his ten-pound-per-week assistant pro salary paid for his lodging with a chap named Butch, who turned out to be gay, and attracted to young David. This inconvenience, added to his being homesick – "no, heartbroken" – resulted in a very short tenure at Mid-Herts. To prevent his homecoming from looking like a total defeat, Feherty bought a car, a 1964 Vauxhall Viva – "monkey-shit brown, and rusted" – and decided to ferry it home. Perhaps having wheels would elevate his status as he came back so soon to Bangor. Not to be: "I hit a pheasant on the drive to the coast, which killed the car," he recalls. "My sister was dating a helicopter pilot at the time. We got him to put it in a sling and drop it in the North Sea."

But Billy Feherty was never discouraged about his only son, and always found something positive to say about him. "Well, the boy is just finding his way," he'd say. "Well, the boy . . ." David returned the favor by not laughing at his father's over-the-top, where-would-you-like-this-sack-of-coal golf swing.

Soon after his carless return home, David took a job at Balmoral Golf Club, a Catholic club in south Belfast. He stayed two years, the most important two years of his life – mostly due to the influence of his boss, the great Fred Daly, who until 2007 was the only Irishman ever to win the Open. Daly, who took the Jug in '47, at Royal Liverpool, and almost won again in '48, was near the end of his thirty years as head professional at the club when Feherty came into his orbit in 1972. The old pro had a square head and gray wavy hair and a tendency to whistle while he worked. And to drink. In his cups, he'd walk through the dining room tossing comic insults at the members while snatching food off their plates, habits so annoying they finally banned him from the clubhouse. Once he sped his orange Hillman Avenger out of the club's parking lot, failed to turn right or left onto Lisburn Road, collided with the gas station across the street, setting one of the pumps on fire – and drove off, apparently not noticing the fireball. "Sir, it's a crime to leave the scene of an accident," the police told him. "That was no accident," Daly replied.

Although his prime had passed when David was in his employ, Daly's immaculate short game had not left him. The old pro's easy-to-lampoon habit while putting was to repeatedly wave his club above the ball while stealing glances at his target, waiting for the right moment to strike, as if the hole had a goalie who might be caught napping. "I have trouble getting out of bunkers," he once told Feherty during one of their rounds together, then splashed his usual artful shot up close to the hole. His assistant pro muttered something. "No, I have trouble getting *out* of fucking *bunkers!*" Daly repeated, scrambling up the steep side of the sandpit on arthritic knees, a little miffed that his meaning had been missed.

Feherty left Balmoral with the foundation of a world-class golf game, an interest in exploring the appeal of alcohol, and a few good stories. Such as: "We hired our caddies based on their entertainment value. I'll never forget Paddy Mooney, with his one shiny shoulder and his two teeth. One day he gets behind a putt I have that obviously breaks a yard or two to the left. He says, 'Play it out two feet to the left.' I say, 'Paddy, come on, that can't possibly be the line.' He looks again and says, 'OK, fock you. One foot.'"

Daly, Balmoral, and caddies who drank their breakfast would find their way into the tales Feherty told at the bar, and later in his "Sidespin" column in *Golf Magazine,* and in his books, and in his speeches after the luncheon. But there were a couple of unhappy memories, too. Twice, violent pacifists or brave cowards or whatever they were detonated the Balmoral clubhouse. The second strike burned it to the ground.

"These were gentleman's bombings, in which the men in ski masks ordered everyone out so no one got killed," Feherty recalls. "They also bombed Shandon Park, Warrenpoint, Belvoir Park . . . probably a dozen golf courses. It wasn't so much about religion. It was about protection money. Money and power."

The years of Feherty's golf career flew past like the road beneath his Porsche. You picture him in his 911, its engine roaring like a jetfighter, the top down, the wind ruffling his dark hair. For almost twenty years he was a fixture on the European Tour, a well-liked fixture who seemed to be enjoying the Bonn-to-Barcelona traveling circus more than anyone. He won ten big events around the world, including the Cannes Open and the Italian Open. He saw money: the pound sterling equivalent of $573,000 over there in 1990, $178,000 in a part-time role in the U.S. in 1994, over $3 million in prize money total. He'd worked his ass off to get a world-class game. His strengths were competitiveness—he was very businesslike on the course—and a short game as immaculate as that of his mentor, Daly. He made the 1991 European Ryder Cup team, and beat reigning U.S. Open champ Payne Stewart in the last-day singles on that hyperdramatic day at Kiawah Island. He married a beauty pageant winner from Johannesburg and lived there for fifteen years. He had a grand time, and he had a drink in his hand when he wasn't cradling a golf club.

But there were problems. The wife was a complainer. Probably he drank too much. Like any golfer not from the United States, he wanted above all things to win The Open—meaning the British Open—and he had the game to do it. But Feherty says he had a self-defeating recessive gene that prevented him from winning the biggest prize. For example: he played exceedingly well in 1989 at Royal Troon, and his name went up on the huge black-on-yellow scoreboard on Saturday night as one of the leaders going into the final round. But they misspelled his name: FARTERY. "Right," he said to himself. "There's your fucking Open champion." Fartery–Feherty shot a final-round 72 when a 68 would have gotten him into the playoff with Greg Norman,

Wayne Grady, and the eventual winner, Mark Calcavecchia. Poor David finished tied for sixth.

In 1994, at Turnberry, Feherty played great again, and knew he was close to the lead with only a few holes left. He remembers looking at a scoreboard near the twelfth green and feeling the odd sensation of fear of success. "I better miss this one," he thought to himself, and he did. Nick Price won; Feherty finished tied for fourth. He'd have had to shoot 65 to catch Nick.

He treated the near misses and the missed cuts and the wins with the same medicine. "People drink heroically in Ireland, especially in Northern Ireland. I'd drink a bottle to get ready to go drink," he says. A few years ago, he quipped, "My parents think my liver is the size of Wyoming."

Self-deprecation and a couple of drinks covered up the agony of his marriage and hid his dark secret moods. "To alcohol," said Homer Simpson once, raising a glass. "The cause of, and the solution to, all of life's problems." But happy or sad, Feherty always had his amazing wit. When his career as a golfer ended in 1997, he hooked up with the media, a match made in heaven. On TV, he was smart enough and confident enough to just keep his mouth shut when the pictures needed no captions, but then his wit revealed itself in brilliant sound bites. His sense of humor in print arrived in ornate and often scatological forms. Here's a sample from his column entitled "Going Mad" in *Golf Magazine* in June 2000, about the aftermath of whacking his golf bag in anger:

> On the next tee, my caddie delved deep for a new ball, only to find I had made solid contact with my Rolex, and a tube of Preparation H, which had spurted out all over

every new ball I had left . . . After about ten minutes, I found the golf ball considerably less irritating and somewhat smaller, which of course meant I hit it farther.

The rise of Feherty coincided with the ascension of Woods, and David has often been assigned by CBS to walk along with Eldrick, to describe the down and distance and the obstacles faced. Tiger often does something godlike, and the announcer often says, while Tiger's cut three iron from a bad lie hangs in the air on its way to a target 280 yards distant, "No one else could have hit that shot." The two are friendly, if not exactly friends, their comfort with each other extending to what Feherty calls their "drive-by farting contest," in which the journalist will lighten the mood but foul the atmosphere by walking near the golfer and letting one rip. Tiger retaliates as space and time (and gas) permit. Feherty took a slight lead to the eighteenth hole during one memorable competition and thought he'd taken the crown. After Woods won the U.S. Open or whatever it was, Feherty offered congratulations. Tiger gripped David's hand, showed those big teeth, and cut a big one. "I win," the new champion said.

From the outside looking in, Feherty looked to have a most delightful life. He remarried, to Anita, and enjoyed raising his two kids, her two, and the one they had together. His books sold. Everyone wanted him to speak at his or her banquet or dinner. Although back problems virtually ended his ability to hit a golf ball, shooting birds and clay targets with shotguns was an absorbing replacement.

But his delightful-appearing life was miserable. "I had this pain and this incredible sadness," he told a reporter in 2006. "I just used humor as a self-defense . . . I felt like most of the time, I was playing the part of me, whatever the hell that is. For a time there, I thought my life was over."

He had clinical depression, a very serious disease not helped by daily dosing with alcohol. He went dry in 2005. "Since I quit drinking and started taking medication, I just feel a million times better," he said. "I know there are millions of people in probably the same position, but they don't know it. Depression is a killer. I think it really helps when people in the public eye come out and say 'Hey, you know what, I suffer from mental illness. But I'm all right. I'm not broken.'"

And more good news: when his sons were being checked for attention deficit disorder, Feherty recalled all the times the thoughts in his head competed for attention like noisy little children. He took the test for ADD, too. He has it, and he's treating it, and he's making up for lost reading time, devouring one book after another. He's even returned to the Shakespeare and Hardy he couldn't digest as a schoolboy.

He sympathizes with American kids who have to read William Faulkner: "Faulkner! Who can get him? Hemingway should have shot Faulkner."

When Feherty faced the very stigmatized problems of alcohol and mental disease, and did so quite publicly, he applied the lesson he learned when his father made him return the paper and pens to his fearsome fourth-grade teacher. "I never forgot that," he says. "You've got to get bad things out in the open, then put them behind you."

Billy Feherty was a good, steady father, but he didn't know about his son's private hell. David didn't want to tell; there was never any soul-baring during the walk between a green and a tee. Nor have games played a crucial role in his interactions with his own children, Erin, Rory, Shey, Karl, and Fred. Golf hasn't made him a better father or made them better kids.

But Feherty's intellectual courage compels him to share his thoughts about another father: God the Father.

He doesn't believe he exists, and when you consider the behavior he observed from the followers of Jesus in Northern Ireland, it's no wonder. "This is the worst time in history to be religious," Feherty says over plates of pasta in a noisy restaurant on a rainy winter day in Dallas. We mutter back and forth about Shias and Sunnis, Arabs and Jews, and the intolerance and intolerable influence of right-wing Christianity in the Supreme Court and on the Presidency of the United States. Wasn't the United States founded by people fed up with official religions?

Yet this nonbeliever does seem to believe in immortality. "When someone hears my daughter laugh, they hear me," he says. "There's a reason for that."

5

FORTY-INCH DRIVER

Doug and A. J. Beechler

Doug Beechler wants to make this perfectly clear: no one—*no one*—will ever hurt or intimidate or take advantage of his son. Doug's a big, easygoing guy, with big, easygoing hair, but his six-foot-four-inch frame straightens for a moment into a vaguely military posture when he tells you they're not going to do to his boy what they did to him.

The tall man became world famous thirty years ago, when he was thirteen. His son, A.J., hovers on the brink of national fame now. "The White Tiger," they call him. He's been on TV several times and in magazines several more. People ask for his autograph. He's six. Father and son were—are—golf prodigies, defining the outer limits of what a kid can do with a good fundamental swing and a perfectly uncluttered mind. They play golf and practice together almost every day and it's not work for either of them. Their joy in each other and in the game they play cannot be missed.

above: A.J. BEECHLER WITH HIS DOTING DAD.

But: *six*. This child has so far to go in golf and in life, and all of it will be flavored by pressure and expectation and by Doug's experience when he looked like the next big thing, and then he wasn't.

"When are we gonna play? Are we gonna play at Wedgwood?" A.J. is all over his father like a $50 suit the moment his dad comes in from another weary day at Frank J. Fazzio and Sons, Inc., purveyors of concrete and concrete accessories in South Jersey. Fazzio and Sons sells bead board, block, brick, steps, stone, and stucco. It rents jackhammers, core drills, vibra screeds, and wet saws. And it mixes, pours, and finishes flowable fill, pump mix, pool mix, and aggregate. Doug oversees the daily logistical nightmare, starting his day at five A.M. so that he can be back home by early afternoon to work with A.J. His vacation will consist of caddying for A.J. in a tournament in North Carolina, where it will be late July and brutally hot. All his discretionary income – and more – goes into A.J.'s golf. "A child, like your stomach, doesn't need all you can afford to give it," a writer named Frank A. Clark once said. Doug Beechler has never heard this quote.

"Wedgwood," Doug says, his weariness gone or forgotten, and soon father and son climb aboard a big black Ford SUV for the ten-minute drive to the golf course. A.J. can't wait; as his father moves the gearshift from D to P, the kid's already out the door. He grabs his clubs and runs like a rabbit through the dusty parking lot to the putting green.

U.S. Kids Golf ranks A.J. the number one six-year-old golfer in the United States. On the abbreviated courses U.S. Kids play (par threes for age six and under are 135 yards or less; par fours are between 145 and 200; and par fives are about 250), A.J. shoots nine-hole scores in the low-to-mid 30s. He's won four of the six tournaments he's played so far in 2006. In July, he won a tournament with a *28*—three eagles, two birdies, four pars. Another of his wins in 2006 came in a playoff. "It was against David Hicks," recalls the little boy. "I hit my drive down the middle and then hit my lob wedge right in the hole." It's his favorite moment in his short career in golf.

August Joshua Beechler's brown eyes widen at the top of his backswing, and his lips purse tightly at impact. Like every golfer, he watches the progress of the ball he's just struck, but he only watches for a moment, because his head abruptly swivels toward his father. There's a lot in this look; at a minimum, it combines *How did I do?* with *Look at me!*

"Good shot!" Doug says most of the time.

"Good" doesn't seem good enough, however, to describe what A.J. does. His setup and grip look terrific, and his striking is solid and powerful with every club. His technique with a driver is most impressive. A.J. swings a two- or three-year-old Ping IS-3 with a handle suitably thin for his little hands, but the club is forty inches long, while he himself is forty-eight inches tall. The equivalent stick for a six-foot-tall man would measure sixty inches, about fifteen inches longer than the standard driver; few golfers could control such a long pole. But with wondrous strength and timing, A.J. sets the club at the top—that is, he finishes his backswing completely—and he attacks the ball from the inside on the way down. He usually hits a bulletlike hook that rolls like crazy when the ground is firm. He can hit it over two hundred, easy. He drives a lot of par fours.

From nearly constant backyard practice, A.J.'s pitching and chipping are excellent. His aggressive technique produces a lot of spin and reminds you of the up-tempo method of Tom Watson in his prime. He's lofted thousands of practice balls into plastic garbage cans. Sand holds no fear, because his dad built a bunker next to the bright green artificial putting surface behind the Beechlers' house on a quiet street in Glassboro, New Jersey.

A.J.'s putting confuses scale; he's so small and close to the ground that when you see him and the hole in the same frame, the cup looks as big as a bucket. He's businesslike with the flat stick, with a firm, uncomplicated stroke that doesn't change whether he's putting for eagle or for bogey. He makes a lot of putts with his two-ball putter and almost makes what he misses. He's still learning to read greens – but you can't know everything in golf before your first day of first grade.

"Take your time and line it up," Doug says, as A.J. is about to plink in a one-footer. We're playing Wedgwood Country Club in Turnersville. The little boy dutifully steps back, lines up, takes a practice stroke, and knocks the tiddler into the cup. During rounds at Wedgwood and Tavistock Country Club in a crazy hot New Jersey July, Doug coaches his son on virtually every shot. Doug's a teaching pro, and a good one, with a vast store of knowledge and a knack for communicating it. And now, he's living a teacher's dream, with a student who is beyond attentive, way past willing – and this perfect pupil is his own son.

A.J.'s mother, Lynne, pitches in, too. Although her background is in tennis, their ritual calls for her to stand with her husband behind their son for pre- and post-shot commentary. Her remarks vary between the obvious ("A little too far left,

A.J.") to the insightful ("You stuck it in the ground that time—don't forget to follow through"). A teacher at a school for profoundly disabled children, she maintains a thorough and well-organized clipping file and log of A.J.'s golf accomplishments. In it, for example, you will learn that A.J.'s birthday is the numerically pleasing 2/20/2000 and that he won the Closest to the Pin competition at the Mayor's Cup at The Birches in Washington Township on June 17, with a shot to twelve-foot six.

An observer is touched by the love and impressed by A.J.'s guileless personality but wonders at the sheer quantity of parental involvement. Shouldn't the child be allowed to absorb golf's lessons of self-sufficiency and self-control? Won't all this help leave him feeling adrift when he has to figure things out for himself? The answers, at least for the moment, are no and no. First of all, the old Scottish game is the unique sport that institutionalized in-competition advisers. They're called caddies. Secondly, U.S. Kids Golf *encourages* mothers and fathers to carry the clubs of their wee bairns.

Involving the family so intimately goes against the grain in junior golf. Anyone who has run a junior tournament will tell you that while they're not as bad as baseball moms and dads taunting your kid to swing and miss, overinvolved golf parents can make you wish you'd remembered your Taser. They slow down play. They want to call penalties on junior's rival. They want a better starting time or a better pairing or free housing closer to the course. They scold, they cajole, they micromanage, and some so obviously put their own egos on the line that they take the game away from the players.

Sometimes, they cheat. With obvious help from his mom, a

kid in a high school tournament in Austin devised a system of semaphore worthy of a third-base coach: if mother held out her left arm, junior should aim left. A hand on her hat signaled that the hole was playing long, so her baby boy should hit an extra club – and so on. The illegally assisted young man consulted a crib sheet to decipher mom's secret code, a square of paper he kept in his pocket with his scorecard. Sweat or karma caused them to stick together, so when he turned in the one the official scorer looked at the other and said, what is *this?*

Another mother, this one in Houston, was busted with a Bushnell rangefinder, a device that measures yardage to targets. At a junior tournament where measuring machines were not allowed, this mom contrived to take readings anyway. "It's one twenty-three, Jimmy," she'd whisper, trying not to let her lips move.

Thus the American Junior Golf Association prohibits in-competition interaction between parents and their children, or even walking very close. One big junior event, the venerable Boys Tournament in Akron, Ohio, has disinvited spectators altogether; mom and dad and college coaches can watch from the clubhouse but that's as close as they can get.

U.S. Kids takes the opposite approach, its goal being to bring families together by the big ones helping the little ones. There's a slightly overt Christian purpose to its program, but nothing in your face. This is fine with Doug Beechler, who often talks about and feels the presence of the Lord. "We want golf to be a family adventure, a relationship sport versus mom or dad's time-away sport," says U.S. Kids Golf founder Dan Van Horn. "That's the ministry part for me." (Van Horn once had an actual ministry on the PGA Tour.) So when Doug and Lynne consult and analyze and direct A.J., they're only doing what they always do in a U.S. Kids tournament.

Team Beechler practices with some urgency. A.J. has qualified for the U.S. Kids Golf World Championship at Pinehurst, North Carolina. The World is only two weeks away. A.J. will be the favorite.

"I'm happy with that one," Doug says. After a bad drive, he's just threaded a four wood around some trees to within thirty yards of the green.

"I'm not," says A.J.

John Corrado, the Beechlers' host at Tavistock, hits another in a series of grounders. "Can I have a mulligan?" he asks A.J. in jest.

"No," replies A.J., definitely not in jest.

Corrado laughs about the exchange a minute later: "You and I are out here putzin' around. But they're *working.*"

"What do you think this one's gonna do?" Doug says, as his student is about to putt. "Think it breaks right? Then aim left. Move your feet. More . . . more . . . too much. There. OK, knock it in . . . Good putt, A."

Doug also calls his son Smurf, Smurfie, Spud, and Buddy.

"What he's good at is imitating," the father says. The faint breeze from riding in the cart provides a momentary respite from the sticky heat. "He'll do whatever you tell him to do. It don't matter, you show him something, boom, he's got it."

A.J. nails his tee shot on the next hole, sprints to the cart piloted by his mother, climbs up on the rear bumper to put his club away, and hops into his seat like a Hollywood stuntman.

"Sometimes when I watch him I get tears in my eyes," Doug says. He's hit his drive about 280; he takes a nine iron from his bag, and smooths it from 153 yards to within 10 feet of the jar. He's got a beautiful grip, a lovely slow rhythm, and he plays a draw. He holes the birdie putt. "I want A.J. to see that I don't just *talk* about golf," Doug says. He might look at playing the fifty-and-older Champions Tour when he's eligible in six years – who knows?

A.J. observes the niceties, standing still when someone else is hitting and waiting his turn to play, but it's plain that he's bursting for the plodding adults to hole out, because then he can practice half a dozen putts before the group proceeds to the next tee. Dad coaches him on every one of these strokes, too.

"He crawled early and he walked early," Doug recalls. "I'll never forget: I was having coffee with my dad, and A.J. crawled up to the table and grabbed the edge and chinned himself up. He listened to us for a few minutes and then let go. He was five months." In one of the Beechler family photo albums, ten-month-old A.J. regards the camera from the pouch of his father's white Ping golf bag like a baby kangaroo. In another shot, he's taking the paper off a club on Christmas morning, and he looks delighted with the gift. He started playing golf at age two.

Back when Doug was teaching full-time at the Pine Canyon driving range in Voorhees, he often took A.J. to work, plunking him down in his car seat in a shady spot close to the lesson tee. He thinks the click and clack of clubs impacting golf balls soothed his infant son. "He wouldn't make a sound while I taught for six, seven hours," Doug says. "Now, when I take him to the range and he hits, he gets a gallery."

Twice during the round at Wedgwood, A.J. is recognized by

people whose backyards abut the golf course. "Aren't you the little boy we saw on TV?" asks a smiling man by the seventeenth green. A.J. nods. "Go over and say hello," Doug says softly. "Go on."

And A.J. walks to the fence and presses the flesh. Then the man's family comes out of the house. They want to meet the child star, too.

In his most recent television appearance, on NBC Channel 10 in Philadelphia, A.J. had been interviewed by a pretty young blonde named Jade McCarthy, who guessed correctly that good TV would result if she took an on-camera lesson from the six-year-old. "Is golf hard?" she asked her instructor. "No," said A.J. She teed up a ball and addressed it. "Don't squat," A.J. said. With an awkward elbows-out swing that suggested a background in field hockey, the reporter hit a dribbler. "That was . . . good," A.J. said diplomatically. "What do you like about golf?" Ms. McCarthy asked. The little boy's eyes went to the tall man standing off camera. "I like him teachin' me," he said.

We finish our round and again A.J. sprints to the putting green to get in a few more licks before it's too dark to see. A hugging, cheek-kissing man of middle years comes out of the twilight, saying, not for the first time, that he'd like to give Doug some cash, to, you know, help with A.J.'s expenses. Doug replies with thanks but no commitment. Something about the man reminds him of the men who "helped" when *he* was the young hotshot twenty-five years ago. They helped themselves, not Doug. Nothing similar will occur to A.J., not as long as his father has something to do with it.

. . .

The Beechler saga began on an easy-to-remember date, 7/6/76, the day Doug shocked New Jersey and the world because of what he did in a junior tournament at his home course, Pitman Country Club.

H. K. Kish, office manager, Ripley's Believe It or Not! Museum of East Forty-fifth Street, New York, New York, became aware of the wondrous feat two and a half months after the fact. H. K. Kish scrolled a piece of letterhead into his IBM Selectric typewriter – you picture him surrounded by Believe It or Not! tchotchkes like shrunken heads and tribal masks – and addressed a letter to the Chamber of Commerce, Williamstown, New Jersey, requesting contact information for "MR. DOUG BEECHLER, a young golfer."

The snippet appeared on March 10, 1977, in the umpteen newspapers across the country that subscribed to Ripley's BION! In the top left of the familiar and oddly irresistible cartoon was a pen and ink drawing of the WORLD'S LARGEST RODENT, the capybara of Eastern Panama and South America, which can attain one hundred pounds in weight and four feet in length. The giant rat seemed to crawl toward the right ear of a portrait of a thoughtful-looking, frock-coated Thomas Carlyle, the nineteenth-century Scottish historian who conducted his five-year courtship of his wife-to-be almost ENTIRELY BY LETTERS (Believe It or Not! believed in all caps). The third part of the daily troika of oddities was an image of a mop-top golfer in full follow-through: "DOUG BEECHLER of Williamstown, N.J., playing golf at the Pitman C.C. in tournament competition, SHOT A 13-UNDER-PAR 58 AT THE AGE OF 13."

No one had ever heard of such a score, especially by someone so young. Numerologists noticed that a thirteen-year-old had shot the thirteen-under 58 and that five plus eight equals thirteen, and that 7/6/76 adds up to thirteen twice. Whatever—Believe It or Not! didn't have the space for any of that.

The first significant occurrence of the incredible day had been Doug banging his noggin against a pipe in the Pitman Country Club cart barn. He worked at the course part-time, but he'd never noticed this particular iron cylinder hanging down from the ceiling next to a battery charger. The resultant headache radiating from the bruise above his right ear bothered him so much that, just before his starting time, he called his mom and asked her to come pick him up. But she told her son to go ahead and try to play. (In keeping with the day's odd symmetry, when Alicia Beechler got Doug's call, she had just come home from work and had gone straight to bed with a migraine.) Doug phoned again after he'd played nine holes. Mom, he said, I'm playing really well. I'm three under. You've got to come down here. So Alicia got to the course and got a cart. In the tenth fairway, he quickly filled her in on his front nine highlights, a birdie and an eagle. Then he birdied the tenth to go four under par.

Doug Beechler was big for his age and wonderfully coordinated for any age. He was the kid the other kids made the captain and the quarterback of any pickup game. He wore checked shorts this day, shin-high white socks, and his lucky red T-shirt, the one with a picture of a reared-up grizzly bear on the front. Beneath the lank blond hair on his hatless head, something wonderful was going on: for four hours, his brain could register only the ball and its targets, and nothing he heard or saw or felt impeded the one thing he was there to do. He birdied the eleventh, the twelfth, the thirteenth, the fourteenth. He pitched in from thirty yards to eagle fifteen. A gallery coalesced, excitement built. As he continued to hit perfect shots and perfect putts, Alicia's emotions welled up, and the effort to hold back tears almost overwhelmed her. But when her son holed out on eighteen, Alicia Beechler let loose a war whoop they could hear in Philadelphia.

Doug had played his second nine in twenty-five strokes, ten under par. Eight birdies and an eagle.

Among other things, he'd lowered the course record by five. The Glassboro *Bulletin* contacted John Fox, a Villanova graduate whose record had been so thoroughly dismissed. "I've never heard of any golfer, amateur or professional, who has covered nine holes in only twenty-five shots," Fox said. "There may be no limit to Doug's overall potential."

Fifty-eight and twenty-five were freak show numbers, so good they were hard to credit, which may be why Believe It or Not! and, later, *The Guinness Book of World Records* picked up the story but *Sports Illustrated* did not. Only one other national publication ran the Beechler piece: *Midnight,* one of the first supermarket tabloids. Alien abductions, Hollywood gossip, and inflating a small fact into a hard-to-believe big deal were the stock-in-trade of the Montreal-based tab; probably its most famous headline was MAN BITES OFF EAR AND EATS IT IN SANDWICH. But *Midnight* played it straight in its coverage of the New Jersey miracle, pointing out the useful fact that the eighteen- and nine-hole records on the PGA Tour were 60 and 27.

"I want to become a professional golfer," the thirteen-year-old told *Midnight*. "I'd like to try now, but I'm not old enough."

Post 58, things were different for Doug Beechler. Teachers and classmates at Williamstown High regarded the only famous person in their midst with new eyes. The school didn't have a golf team but one was quickly organized, and a coach assigned. "What I remember is that he could chip and putt with anybody," recalls Doug's coach, John Jingehino, who is now seventy-nine. "And that he spent half his life at that Pitman golf course." Doug was allowed to hit practice balls while the other kids went through the same old calisthenics and games in gym class. But sometimes he thought of the 58 as a mere fluke, and his elevated status clashed with his adolescent desire to fit in.

You could see the ambivalence in a photograph taken after his monumental achievement, when Doug and his pro and mentor Charles Lepre posed for the newspaper. Lepre, a handsome, wavy-haired gentleman who often affected a shirt and tie, held up the famous scorecard. The man and the boy and the rectangle of paper formed a tableau just like that staple of the small-town newspaper, the big fish story—LOCAL YOUTH CATCHES RECORD CATFISH IN LAKE CLARK—except that instead of wearing a grin, the Local Youth looked dour, even suspicious.

"Doug was very unassuming," recalls his father. "No puffed-up ego or attitude. People had to probe to get his accomplishments out of him."

"It was awkward," Doug says. "I didn't think a whole lot of it (the 58). It embarrassed me to talk about it, really. It meant more to others than to me. I still wanted to have fun . . . I didn't understand the repercussion."

Doug says things remained the same at home: "Dad was the worker. Mom did the tournaments."

August Martin "Gus" Beechler ran a lithograph machine for thirty years at the nearby Owens-Illinois factory. He took up golf on a day when he had childcare duty, so he handed five-year-old Doug a club and a ball and parked him in the practice field next to the golf course. This worked pretty well for all concerned, so they did it again and again. Father and son got serious about golf at about the same time. Gus would come home from the factory and hit balls. For spending money, he caddied at Pine Valley. "That's where I got my work ethic from," Doug says, "watching him." In time, little Doug was invited to play in his father's group on weekends. The grown men gambled, and made the boy part of the bet. Doug knew he had to perform. Because of this training, he says, there wasn't a golf tournament that could scare him. But the experience also made him feel used.

"The only regret I have about those days is that my sister Tracy got put on the back burner," Doug says. "Ninety percent of the time it was Doug-this and Doug-that. I feel really, really bad about that. I'd give my life for my sister."

Post 58, doors opened. Several dozen savvy college golf coaches put Doug Beechler on their radar and prepared their recruiting pitches. Girls noticed him a little more. A better class of junior golf tournament asked him to play in their events – such as the White Rose Invitational in York, Pennsylvania, where he competed against future Tour pros Bobby Clampett and Mark Calcavecchia, and beat them. He won the White Rose three years in a row. He won the South Jersey Junior four years in a row. Doug estimates that he'd won three hundred junior tournaments by the time he was sixteen, which sounds hyperbolic, but there's no question he had a bigtime game.

He reached his private summit in July 1979.

Three years almost to the day after he got into *Guinness,* Doug shot 74-66 to set tournament and course records in the New Jersey Insurance Youth Classic at Forsgate Country Club. But that was nothing: a couple of days later, he became (probably) the youngest person ever to qualify for a PGA Tour event. "Probably" because the Tour does not keep an official youngest-ever record, and, for some reason, Doug Beechler is not in their database. No one at Tour headquarters can remember a younger qualifier than Ty Tryon, who had attained sixteen years and nine months when he played his way into the 2001 Honda Classic. (Michelle Wie, the youngest to hit a shot in a Tour event—she was fourteen years, two months, and twenty-nine days when she teed off in the 2004 Sony Open—did not qualify. She was invited. Likewise for Tiger Woods; when he played in the 1992 Nissan Open six weeks after his sixteenth birthday; he got in on a sponsor's exemption.)

So here is news for the PGA Tour: at age fifteen years, eleven months, and a few days, Doug Beechler was the youngest ever to qualify for one of its tournaments.

Tour qualifiers have a uniquely nerve-wracking vibe, so when Doug shot a 72 and won a two-hole playoff for the last spot, beating scores of local pros and "rabbits" (vernacular for the dreamers from all over the world who chased the tour and a buck by playing in what were then simply called Mondays) he made a powerful statement. Considering the competition and the stakes, it was in its way a bigger deal than the 58. He'd made the field of the 1979 IVB Classic at Whitemarsh Valley Country Club in Philadelphia. He'd be competing against Nicklaus, Player,

Strange, and Crenshaw, and he wouldn't turn sixteen for three more weeks. Who could argue that the kid from South Jersey was the best young golfer in the world?

Perhaps it's harsh but it seems to be true: at this point, things started to not work out for Doug Beechler. An amorphous enemy emerged – the "they" that he will protect A.J. from at any cost.

Jack Nicklaus came out of the cool locker room to stand in the usual Whitemarsh cauldron with hundreds of others to watch the youngest qualifier in Tour history hit his first shot. Alicia Beechler sneaked a peak at her son's idol as his name was announced – yes, Jack joined in the applause. Doug had also noticed the Bear but he didn't seem to care. He looked down the fairway. Mature oaks and maples guarded the left side of the tenth hole and freshly painted white stakes protected the right. With that trouble, plus bunkers and a narrow landing area, and given that it was only 380 yards long, most competitors laid up with a cut two or three iron. Spectators in the amphitheater were so close they could almost hear the players breathe, and vice versa. But Doug ignored every reason for caution. He took a three wood – and killed it down the middle.

Twenty or so people marched in the Beechler gallery, energized by the moment but enervated by the saturated heat. Out front was Coach Jingehino, a baseball and football star back at Trenton State, and still in good shape; then the proud parents, Gus and Alicia; the equally proud pro, Lepre; Denise De Pasquale, Doug's show-stopping girlfriend; and a dozen of his buddies from school. The blond-haired boy looked nerveless for the first three holes, but then he got a break bad enough to dent anyone's composure. His second shot on the par-four thirteenth rolled over the green and into the rough, which the marshal on duty marked by placing a towel next to the ball – or so he thought. Doug chopped out of the deep soft grass but when he marked his ball, he discovered that it wasn't his. The mortified marshal checked the verdure again. *Oh. Here's your ball. Sorry.* But sorry didn't matter – the penalty was two shots. Doug had a double bogey and a persecuted feeling. Yet when he hit it in the rough on the fifteenth, and one of his homeys pointed at the ball and said, "Make sure it's yours, Doug," he was able to laugh.

Lou Graham won. Nicklaus tied for third, Crenshaw tied for eighth, and Player missed the cut by one. Doug's 84-79 missed the cut by twenty.

But it had been a good experience overall, and hardened Doug's desire to play the Tour. The 84-79 was soon forgotten, because the Beechlers had another number to worry about. Forty-eight – or was it forty-nine? – colleges and universities had offered Doug a scholarship. All the big golf schools stood in line, including Wake Forest, the alma mater of Arnold Palmer, another of Doug's heroes. Based mostly on the certainty of warm weather, he chose Florida State. A fiasco. He lasted just seventeen days in Tallahassee. Each day, while hitting practice balls at the university golf course, one of the pros would approach and say, "let's get those hands a little higher" or something – but Doug didn't feel his swing needed fixing, and as a seventeen-year-old out on his own for the first time, he lacked the chutzpah to tell the pro to go back inside the clubhouse and leave him the hell alone. "I called my mom and said, 'This is not for me,'" he recalls. "I didn't really want to go to college anyway. I just wanted to get my card and go play."

The card never came. His glory fading, Doug played amateur golf for a couple of years, supporting himself, as always, by working for Charlie Lepre at Pitman Country Club. Bigshot friends recruited him a couple of times for Calcuttas; they made money betting on the birdie machine, but didn't share their winnings as they'd promised, and didn't even pick up his expenses. He turned pro, and almost immediately got in Dutch with the Philadelphia Section of the PGA of America, for playing in tournaments it did not sanction. The PGA revoked his membership. Doug got back in, and he's been a member for twenty years, but he and the Philadelphia Section have never seen eye to eye.

"In Florida, I was playing against (the current Tour professionals) Skip Kendall and Lenny Mattiace, and their games were no different than mine," Doug recalls. "Although I didn't get it in the hole as well. The one thing that bothered me was going from bent grass to those slow Bermuda greens."

On a misty day in the late fall of 1983, the twenty-year-old pro was in his blue Mazda XR-6 driving south on Highway 49 near Millville, New Jersey, heading for I-95 and Florida and another series of mini-tour events. His plans changed very suddenly: a green northbound Mack tractor-trailer came around a corner, skidded, and jackknifed, heading for the little Japanese car with frightening speed. The Mazda swerved to the right into someone's yard. Doug ducked. Wham! The truck passed through and directly over the car – he thinks he would have been decapitated if he hadn't lowered his head – and the trailer ended up directly on top of the flattened XR-6. He never lost consciousness. Time dragged as he lay pinned in the deformed blue metal, feeling the pain of crushed ribs, a mangled left shoulder, and a twisted back. He heard sirens, and voices, and the whir of a saw cutting him out of his coffin.

The trucking company had a better lawyer; the settlement barely paid the injured golf pro's medical expenses. Nothing for lost wages. And they tried to give *Doug* a ticket—for not wearing a seatbelt. That charge was thrown out of court but the insult still burns.

Recovery seemed to take forever: "A year and a half after the accident, I was playing with my father in a team thing. I hit my drive on the fifth or sixth hole and one of my ribs came out of its cup and right into my lung. I could not move. They had to come out and get me. The pain—it was like having the wind knocked out of you only ten times worse. And the feeling of three doctors pushing the rib back in place was even worse than that." The injuries still affect the way he swings.

He played the mini-tours in New England and Florida for eight years with some success but without a win. At age thirty, he circled back to Pitman, site of the 58, as the head pro. He worked there for nine years. He had three kids and one divorce. While giving a lesson in 1995, a student took an unexpected swing and whacked Doug solidly in the fingers of his right hand. He wore a cast for three years.

When the 1990 *Guinness Book of World Records* mentioned Doug, it misspelled his surname, leaving out the *L*.

But it wasn't all bad luck and trouble for Doug Beechler. After all, he met the beautiful blonde Lynne Fazzio at the driving range and married her in '99. A year later, they had A.J.

. . .

A.J. finished third at the U.S. Kids Worlds. "He hit the ball super," Doug says, "but he couldn't get used to the slow greens." He shot 37-35-36 and finished three shots behind a big kid from Texas who could drive the par fives.

But third out of eighty of the best little golfers in the world was hardly a failure, and other aspects of the event were an unqualified success. A.J. hunted turtles in a Pinehurst water hazard and caught a couple. He splashed in the Holiday Inn swimming pool with other little golfers from around the world. He learned to say *konichi-wa.* And this, recalled by Doug: "We're at the opening ceremonies at this high school stadium, and there are 4,500 people and parachutists and the flags of the world. From the stage, they say, 'We got results from the Skills competition.' We're not thinkin' nothin' of it. They say, 'The six-and-under champion is A.J. Beechler.' He jumped five feet. The expression on his face! Ear-to-ear grin."

For A.J. to play in the Worlds, Lynne and Doug had spent their vacations and several thousand dollars on gasoline, hotel, and meals. Was it worth it? Are you kidding?

"He is the light of my eye," Doug says. "He and my wife are everything to me. Last week, I gave him a gap wedge, and it was like I'd given him the world. He gave me a big, big, tight hug, and it felt like the Lord coming down and putting his hand on my back and saying, 'Way to go, that's what it's about.'

"My parents did a great job. They never pushed me, they put up with me, they gave me time, even gave me money my first year as a pro—but I want to do it better. Ten times better. I want A.J. to have so much fun in life."

Will his father's loving golf guidance be the key to this happiness? What will happen if A.J. decides gymnastics floats his boat? Or cars or girls or NASCAR—or nothing? Stupid question. The Beechlers are not thinking that way, they're dealing with this opportunity they've got now, not planning for the unlikely or the unpredictable. They're contemplating a move from New Jersey to Pinehurst, where the people are so nice, and A.J. can play his game year-round.

6

CROSS-HANDED

Bill and Jeffrey Wolff

The greatest tennis player in history stared at the air, so deep in thought he looked hypnotized. The blond, thin-faced man adjusted his socks, shoelaces, and sweatbands. He touched the grips of his rackets. If Rod Laver heard the muffled public address announcements through the dressing room walls he gave no sign; nothing penetrated his trance. Will Rogers Coliseum in Fort Worth usually hosted concerts, rodeos, and horse shows, but tonight the white lines and net of a makeshift tennis court gleamed in the light, an exciting novelty.

Applause crackled as Laver and his friend and rival Ken Rosewall entered the arena. Trailing them were two local amateurs, both of whom had played college tennis at a high level and were now, at about age forty, pillars of the community. Ted Gorski Jr., from the University of Texas, was an attorney and the vice president of a Dallas bank. Billy Wolff, an SMU alum, practiced general surgery

above: JEFFREY WOLFF AND THE AZALEA-DOGWOOD QUEEN AT THE FUTURE MASTERS, DOTHAN, ALABAMA, 1980.

in Fort Worth. Several thousand fans and friends bought tickets to see the show and to benefit the charity, the Lena Pope Home.

Laver-Gorski beat Rosewall-Wolff in three sets and then the doctor, the lawyer, and the Australian tennis pros shook hands and retreated to the locker room. Of all the elements of the experience – the feeling of playing in front of a big, loud crowd, and the way the Aussies consistently hit lines and corners with hard shots – Wolff had been most impressed with the way Laver covered himself in concentration as if it were a coat. He kept the coat on, even in the aftermath. The physician, an ebullient sort, aimed a few lighthearted comments at the great man as they toweled off – How do you hit that topspin forehand so hard? Were you *trying* to ace me with your second serve? – but got nothing but grunts and monosyllables from Rod "The Rocket" Laver, and a look as if he'd tasted sour milk.

Wolff thought about that nonconversation for years. Laver's demeanor further convinced him that tennis – like other sports, like life – is ultimately a mental game. Persistence and adaptability had always been the sharpest arrows in his own quiver, not his serve or his backhand or anything he did physically. Billy Wolff made his opponents understand that he had prepared for pretty much every shot and stratagem they might throw at him and that he'd quickly adjust to anything he hadn't expected. Persistence and adaptability got him a college scholarship, and to and through medical school, and twice to the quarterfinals of the NCAA Championship. He beat the 1963 Wimbledon singles champion Chuck McKinley in a college match, probably his high-water mark; who you defeat is the gold standard in tennis, not where and certainly not how.

Wolff never considered turning pro and never regretted not having the experience. Besides the fact that he had a wife and two kids by the time he was a senior in college, and a career in medicine waiting, he knew that the top players surpassed him physically and mentally. But in time he found a competitive mind as strong as any he'd ever seen. It belonged to his seven-year-old son. When his boy prepared to hit a golf ball, his focus and emotional control were so complete that the world went away. He hit perfect shot after perfect shot. When he was four, they put him in a tournament. When it was over, the little boy penciled a wobbly *X* on his scorecard because he couldn't yet sign his name. He won the tournament.

Then he won lots of tournaments. Who you defeat is not as important in golf as it is in tennis, but it became hard to ignore that Jeffrey Wolff was beating *everyone* his age, including that slight boy from Dallas, Justin Leonard, and the slim lefty from Southern California, Philip Mickelson, and the sturdy, impassive youngster from Florida, David Duval. The whippings Jeff put on Justin, Phil, and David were no joke, but the *way* he did it seemed like a punch line.

He gripped the club cross-handed. The best little golfer in the USA held the club upside down.

Dr. William Wolff had a prodigy on his hands.

What should a dad do when his child shows an unusual talent? Should his other kids stand in the background? Should he? Music history provides two of the best-known examples of fathers and their little geniuses.

Mozart's daddy sat his son down at the clavier at age three

and didn't let him get up. "The iron shirt of discipline," one biographer called it; little Wolfgang liked the fit. Leopold Mozart's ambition for his son may have been a product of and a reaction to his own career, but Mozart Senior was no failure. His book of violin instruction was very well received, as were his numerous orchestral compositions; he rose to second in command – vice-Kapellmeister – of the court orchestra in Salzburg, Austria. Possibly his achievements were not as grand as he'd hoped. That only two of the seven Mozart children survived beyond infancy could further explain Leopold's extreme involvement with his youngest. Money surely motivated him; you didn't get rich on his assistant choir director's salary, and musicians had only the social status of any of the other servants of the court. Another aspect of his parental attitude is not in doubt, because he said it often: Leopold Mozart felt that God had selected him to help his child.

So perhaps it was God's will when Wolfgang was six and the family left for a concert tour of Europe – and didn't come home for almost three and a half years. His father and his mother Anna Maria were the tour's booking agents, publicists, and roadies. The incredible composing boy and his older (by five years) sister Maria Anna played two shows a day most days – keyboard and violin, usually, and compositions by masters such as Bach or something the little genius had written himself. Sometimes dad joined in. They received one hundred ducats per performance from the powdered wigs at Versailles and Buckingham Palace, a little less from lesser nobility. When cash ran low, as it did in England, Wolfgang and his sister played three-hour gigs at inns. It all worked, and Mozart became immortal, mostly due to his talent but partly, according to mozartproject.org, because he "enjoyed the extra attention, and found great pleasure in learning—and in pleasing his father."

The pleasing-his-father business went on all their lives. Leopold manipulated the relationship by parceling out the approval and affection his son craved.

From Bonn, Germany, Herr Beethoven watched. Like Leopold Mozart, Johann Beethoven was a court musician—a tenor, violinist, and keyboard player. And like Herr Mozart, he had a son with great potential. But his boy "did not learn very much at school," according to a contemporary account. "That is why his father so early seated him at the clavier and kept him at it so severely." Johann put his brilliant Ludwig on stage for the first time when he was seven, while billing him for box office purposes as his "little son of six years." Ludwig's formal education ended at age ten.

Although Johann devoted himself to his son's musical training, and got him lessons with the best teachers, he didn't capitalize as efficiently as Mozart's daddy did. For one thing, Ludwig wasn't as advanced as Wolfgang had been at the same age (Mozart was nineteen years older than Beethoven). And for another, Johann was a booze bag. Often he came home after the bars closed to pull Ludwig out of bed for a music lesson or for a performance, for himself and a friend, usually on the violin. Most biographers hint or state plainly that Herr Beethoven also beat his son. In any case, it's impossible to separate the father's heavy hand from his son's tortured life—and his brilliance.

When his father's alcoholism worsened, Ludwig took over the support of the family, beginning at age eighteen. He was unusually independent. And unlike every other notable composer/musician before him, Ludwig van Beethoven did not submit to an employer. A musical freelancer, he sold his compositions, took money from patrons, and in performance settings similar to poetry slams, he won every piano-off by knockout. But by age thirty, he started to go deaf, and had no one to comfort him, because his love life was a permanent mess. He always went after the wrong woman, and he never married. Depression stole the joy from his life off and on for years. He also suffered from chronic nausea, lack of appetite—a general distress he called "kolik." Modern analysis of hair samples taken from the composer's head reveals that he probably suffered from lead poisoning. Lead was everywhere back then, in the cups one drank from and even in the wine in the cup. And poor frustrated, depressed, wifeless, childless Ludwig drank a lot of wine, possibly as much as his father had. He died from liver failure.

Yet the music this man made two hundred and fifty years ago continues to soar and inspire. Did Beethoven succeed in spite of, or because of, his father?

Hollywood weighed in on the complicated prodigy-parent subject with *Little Man Tate,* a film directed by and starring Jodie Foster (who was herself an acting and modeling wunderkind who debuted as the Coppertone kid at age three). The movie involves a loving but somewhat doltish single mom—played by Ms. Foster—who allows her seven-year-old son to be boarded at a school for geniuses. The child thrives for a while in the company of other kids who can instantly calculate the cube root of an eight-digit number or build a functioning sump pump with half a box of ziti. But what about his emotional needs? Mom is conflicted. The Little Man, whose intellect isolates him on his best day, begins to feel imprisoned. He has no father except an absent biological one, and his father figure, played by Harry Connick Jr., disappoints. In the film's big finish, the boy genius intentionally tanks an interview on network TV, refusing to discuss god symbols in Dostoyevsky, giving instead the false impression that Dr. Seuss is more his taste. He goes back to mom, and normal schooling, and a normal life. It's a happy ending.

Academics have also studied and dissected prodigiousness, of course, but it's too slippery a subject for science to grip. They've figured out almost nothing on the biology part. The most thorough and famous effort by the academy was the Lewis Terman project, begun in 1921 and lasting for seventy years, which evaluated the lives of fifteen hundred California children with IQs above 140. The kids in the Terman study proudly called themselves Termites. Certain aspects of their relationships with their mothers were part of the analysis, but in 1921 fathers, apparently, were not thought to be worth considering—so there's no data on the dads.

Terman determined that children could excel at a very high level where the rules were most clear, such as in chess, music, and some sports. That the fifteen hundred Termites would eventually write two hundred books and receive three hundred fifty patents is no surprise. Nor is the floundering many of the bright kids endured in adulthood, and the mental illness, alcoholism, and twenty-two suicides.

The case of Randy seems particularly poignant. Starting at age five, little Randy regularly wrote plays—they all had superhero protagonists, but still. In time, however, he faced the fate of many or most prodigies: the other kids caught up. In high school, there were plenty of playwrights as good as he was, a fact Randy found hard to accept. He wasn't special anymore.

Social scientists who review the Lewis Terman data conclude, among many other things, that early promise is no predictor of later success, and that parents who push too hard are setting up their children for a fall.

"Get it, get it, run, GOOD!" the man says. "That's it, go, go, go, GOOD!" It's August first, and it's 105 degrees in north central Texas, and Dr. William Wolff is running my ass off.

We're at the beautiful Bayard-Friedman tennis complex at Texas Christian University. Around the sunken, live-oak sheltered courts, workers work in super slow motion, dragging rakes and pulling weeds. Other maintenance employees in green uniforms sit in the sultry shade with their backs up against the pro shop, smoking and talking quietly *en español.* Their eyes follow the two white men who are voluntarily running in this insane heat, and they must think, how stupid.

We warm up – warm up! – in the usual way, with groundies, volleys, overheads, serves. No one says, "Let's play a set," but points break out. Wolff is thirteen years older than I but his anticipation is so good, and my shots are apparently so predictable, that almost nothing gets past him. Spinning balls hit right at his shoes he half-volleys with ease. His ground strokes arrive dependably deep and, when he wants to win one of our impromptu points, in corners or on lines.

And yet he's encouraging and upbeat every minute. "That's it, get it, run, run, NICE TRY!" He compliments my athleticism and fitness, neither of which is all that great. He mentions during a break, while my shoulders heave and his do not, that inside his incredibly young-looking legs he's got replacement knees of titanium and plastic, and that following his surgery on December 13, 2005, he gained one and a half inches in height, so bowed had his legs been. He's got brown eyes, a deep tan, a full head of gray hair, and he doesn't wear a hat in this pitiless sun. He uses an empty tennis ball container as a drinking glass. Old School.

Dr. Wolff is a general surgeon—just retired—which calls to mind the stereotypes of the different medical specialists. Just watch the TV show *Scrubs* or ask any med student: pathology and radiology attract those who aren't good with patients. Dermatologists are smart, with nights and weekends free, for rare is the emergency call for rashes or zits. Internists are nerds prone to god complexes. Surgeons are the most fun—optimistic to the point of being gung-ho, and self-assured to the point of being insufferable. They're often jocks. What must it have been like to be a gifted athlete and the son of this particular surgeon? Did this almost-tennis-pro drill his sure-to-be-a-golf-pro son in heat like this, as enthusiastically as this? Did he see his child as part of the Mozart-Beethoven-Laver continuum?

We'd met two hours before in cooler circumstances. The Wolffs live in a pretty—and pretty expensive—neighborhood in Fort Worth, with creeks and hills relieving the endemic flatness of north central Texas. August heat bakes the wood shingle roof of the Wolffs' house to the point of combustion but inside it feels like the bottom drawer in a refrigerator. Bill and his lovely wife Gail chat easily and amiably about family history and Jeff and golf and so on, but the surgeon is a sunburst of restless energy, and he makes it plain that we're not going to just sit here and talk all day. He's wearing tennis shorts and shoes; he intends to play as soon as his guest runs out of questions.

"Golf? No, I'm too hyped up to play golf," says Dr. Wolff. "Although I am a pretty good golfer. I played at Worth Hills, that old muni course – and I won some money from Dan Jenkins, and that other writer, Strake. Shrake? Bud Shrake. Ask 'em. But I gave up golf my junior year and won the city high school singles in tennis and made it to the quarters in State. Went to SMU on a partial scholarship back in the days when freshmen were not eligible to play, so I practiced hitting tennis balls on the handball court all winter and then I beat everyone on the team. I made All-American twice and won the Southwest Conference once. I was number one singles for three years and had a full scholarship. Premed."

Gail met Bill at Methodist Hospital in Houston. She was a cardiac intensive care nurse with a calm disposition and a good backhand. He was a surgeon just out of residency, wired as three cups of coffee, divorced, and the father of three – Shane, then eleven; Peter, eight; and Katie, age seven. That was okay with Gail – she liked kids. But Shane, Peter, and Katie lived with *him,* full-time. Gail took a deep breath and jumped into the deep end of the marital pool. Three years later, in May 1972, Jeffrey was born.

In the summer of '74, while his parents played mixed doubles at Colonial Country Club, Jeff puttered around on the other side of the fence, on a wonderland of perfectly maintained, brush-cut grass. At some point, the blond-haired boy compared the simple earnest fun of golf practice to the sweaty minuet on the tennis court. Several magic moments occurred in quick succession: he picked up a club, not a racket; he held it with his left hand on the bottom, as if it were a shovel, and wrapped his thumbs around the grip, as if it were a rope; he swung; and thrilled to the sweetness, the wholeness of his first solid hit. It went so far and he could control it. He was hooked. Hypnotized.

The slightly less cinematic truth of the birth of Jeff's golf game is that he'd been picking up clubs and rackets cross-handed since the time his age was measured in months (he held a crayon or a spoon right-handed, but threw a ball lefty; some equate ambidexterity with genius). At age two, while swinging his sawed-off Arnold Palmer putter in the house, he accidentally impaled the family dog. "Got him right in the chest, gave him a pneumothorax," Bill Wolff recalls. "But we didn't tell him he'd killed Nicky." So Jeff's fondness for holding a golf club remained undisturbed. At age two, he would putt for the two hours it took his parents to play three sets. At four, he was whacking out five large buckets of balls with his fairway wood, an exertion requiring several hours. At five, he was given a special exemption to play the course. It was nothing for him to stay on the practice green for entire mornings or afternoons. "Roland Harper (the golf professional) would draw a crowd," Bill recalls. "He'd say, 'Watch this kid putt. *This* is how to putt.'

"Jeff had a real unusual talent. He was tremendously focused and he worked so very hard. I thought he was every bit as good as Tiger . . . I remember him playing thirty-six holes and then coming home to fall asleep in front of the TV."

Such talent and effort had to be supported, Jeff's parents decided. They would not be in-your-face disciplinarians, like the fathers of Beethoven and Mozart. There was no need; from DNA or imitation, the son worked at golf the way the father worked at tennis. Nor would they make money off of Jeff—that was impossible, anyway. And while they felt a great deal of pride in their son, there was no hint of Herr Beethoven's creepy desire for reflected glory. No: the Wolffs would support Jeff simply, by making sure the game was always available to him. Not so much with lessons, although he had a few, and not with nightly golf games, because Bill and Gail stuck to tennis. Their gift to Jeff was time and money, two commodities Bill's parents had been unable to provide his nascent tennis career. *His* father never attended a match.

"Mom watched a few—very few," Wolff recalls. "If I won six-one, six-one, she'd ask me why I gave up so many games . . . But it wasn't that they were disengaged. Dad was just working all the time (for the post office) and they had their own printing business. I remember them stuffing envelopes, even on Sunday."

The family would go to Albuquerque or Tulsa or Quincy, Illinois, for a junior tournament and call it their summer vacation. Other days it was take Jeff to the course, pick him up from the course, take him back again, pay his bill for range balls . . . No one minded. Jeff's utter consistency was in fact a pleasant given in an often chaotic household. "A lot of hassle in the house," Bill says. But Gail recalls no jealousy or resentment at all the attention Jeff got as the different elements in the family tried to blend. On the contrary—Shane, Peter, and Katie loved that their step-sib was in the paper and on TV.

TV? Yes, starting at age four. Jeff Wolff was a media star from the start, an irresistible combination of precociousness and elfin cuteness. And that grip. Sample headlines:

HITTING BALLS CROSS-HANDED NO HANDICAP
FOR 8-YEAR-OLD GOLFER

UNORTHODOX GRIP HELPS CLOSE GAP

UNIQUE APPROACH GETS GOOD RESULTS

CROSS-HANDER HAS GRIP ON HIS GAME

FORT WORTH JUNIOR GOLFER IN HUNT,
ANY WAY HE SWINGS AT IT

WOLFF ENJOYING SUCCESS
DESPITE CROSS-HANDED APPROACH

At age seven, playing in the eleven-and-under division, he won the North-South Junior by five. That same summer, he won the Texas-Oklahoma Junior ten-and-unders by thirteen. In seven events as a nine-year-old, he won five. His margins of victory in the stroke play events that summer were four, six, thirteen, and —wait for it—*nineteen.* He hit the ball better and, with his wristy whirlwind of a swing, much, much farther than other kids his age. Winning proves superior focus, and often a more disciplined mind, and so it was with Jeff.

He also liked doing things *right.* So frequently did he call penalties on himself for infractions no one else had seen that his father suspected a mental defect. He took Jeff to a psychologist. Just a very honest, meticulous kid, the shrink said. Live with it. "When he was eight, at the Future Masters in Dothan, Alabama, he'd finished his round and we're back at the hotel," Dr. Wolff recalls. "Jeff's all worried, because he remembered that he'd marked his ball on one green, but now he thinks he might actually have been on the fringe. We took him back to the course – can you imagine this little eight-year-old doing this? – and he explains his case to a tournament official. 'Will you abide by our decision?' the official says, and Jeff nods yes. Well, he wasn't disqualified, and it was such a weight off his shoulders that the next day he shot a nine-hole record that lasted ten years."

One day the precocious boy went across town to play at Shady Oaks Country Club. And when the greatest retired golfer in the world saw him swing, and how well he hit the ball, he did something he *never* did: he interrupted his lunch. Because from his perch overlooking the practice range and ninth and eighteenth greens, he observed this rail-thin kid zinging out balls with the same grip *he'd* used the first time he picked up a club. "He and Hogan played a couple of holes," Bill recalls. "Jeff came home all excited. 'I gave him your number and he said he'd call.'"

For a while the Wolffs had some slight expectation that the great man would tutor their tyro, but Ben went back to his lunch and stayed there. Later, when Jeff began to suffer a general golf malaise, he took a couple of lessons from well-thought-of instructors, all of whom advised a switch to a conventional grip. Jeff didn't switch. Couldn't, wouldn't.

Bill Wolff contacted David Leadbetter, who had become the doorman outside a nightclub called Get Rich and Famous Playing Golf. The Wies (Michelle), the Howells (Charles III), the Granadas (Julieta, she of the $1 million winners check in the ADT Championship in November 2006), and others traveled to

Leadbetter's Florida headquarters to find out if their child's name was on the list. Jeff Wolff, who had just turned thirteen in May 1985, flew to Orlando by himself.

When the instructor saw Jeff hit a ball, his mind skipped to one of the most important but obscure figures in golf history: Sewsunker "Papwa" Sewgolum. A South African of Indian descent and a former caddie, he won the 1963 Natal Open, a big deal made bigger because the great Harold Henning was in the field. Sewgolum took this same provincial tournament in 1965, and this time the '65 U.S. Open champion Gary Player competed. Sewsunker played cross-handed; that was interesting. His skin was brown; that was a problem. Because when they began the trophy presentation in '65, it began to rain, and then to pour, and everyone scurried into the clubhouse – everyone but the guest of honor. Here was apartheid in action: if Durban Country Club allowed a dark-skinned person inside its clubhouse, it would lose its liquor license. Photos of the drenched golfer holding a trophy went around the world with a caption explaining the circumstances. The image caused an outcry. A number of countries announced they would no longer allow their sports teams to compete in or with a nation that perpetrated such a shameful practice. Seemingly in retaliation for the commotion he'd created, the next year the South African government withdrew Papwa's permission to play golf with whites, and then it took away his passport. He died poor, before age fifty. Heart.

Leadbetter is a South African, and knows this story well. He was the first instructor Jeff ever met who didn't try to change his grip. Besides, "he was hitting it great," Leadbetter says. "There was no need to move his hands." Instead they concentrated on flattening his swing plane. But Jeff didn't change. Couldn't, wouldn't. He had his own way.

Jeff's unusual self-containment revealed itself in another way that week, when he called his mom to say that he was having such a good time that he'd like to stay a few days more. Well, Gail said, trying one of those experiments parents often attempt on their kids: someone will have to change your plane and hotel reservations and your shuttle to the airport. If you want to handle all that, go ahead. "OK," Jeff said. Gail put down the phone. "Willy," she said in amazement to her husband, "I think he's gonna do it." He did.

In the cool house on the hot day you balance one of Jeff's thick scrapbooks on your knee, and then another. You read familiar names – James Furyk of Mannheim, PA – and then you wonder, where are you, Jay Pennypacker of Mesa, AZ? And you, Keith Sbarbo of San Diego, and you, Anthony Andrews of Kokomo, IN? What ever happened to Nicky Goetze of Hull, GA, and Luis Felipe del Solar of Lima, Peru? Golf's brutal winnowing process turned them all into Randy, the kid who wrote plays.

Finally, amidst the numbing sportswriterese – "uses a funny-looking cross-handed grip but still ranks No. 1 among the country's 11-and-under shotmakers" – you find the moments that start to explain one of the prodigies, and maybe most of them.

At age sixteen, in 1988, in the twelfth year of his competitive career, Jeff had his first summer without a win. Rounds of 69 and 70 were only good enough for second place in a high school tournament. He shot 75, 74, 74 at an American Junior Golf Association event in New Orleans – fourth place. Little Jeff was becoming Much Bigger Jeff: a growth spurt of four inches and twenty-five pounds brought him to six foot two and 160 pounds. "What's going on with you?" a reporter asked. "I don't know," Jeff answered. "I guess it's harder now because the courses are harder, playing the back tees all the time. And the competition is a lot harder. When I was ten and eleven I hit it a lot farther than the other boys my age. They weren't even close. I'd enter tournaments and I'd know I was going to win. It was real easy."

Car keys symbolize the decline and fall of most golf prodigies. Not so with Jeff; he didn't start hanging out at the mall or a girl's house or the auto parts store. His obvious problem was putting – bitter irony for the one-time king of the practice green – but other, less concrete things weighed him down. Longevity, for one: as has been often observed, it's rare for an athlete to remain at the top for more than ten years. It applied to Hogan, Palmer, Nicklaus, and Laver; and now it applied to Jeff, who had been about the best around from age four to fourteen.

"He'd been spending five and six hours on the practice green, an absolute *robot.* But then, that stopped," Bill Wolff recalls. "When he started slipping, I started pushing him a little bit. I may have mishandled that . . . I'd say, 'You've got to go out and putt.' He'd say, 'Dad, you don't get it. There's more to life than putting.'"

There's a long silence in the room. "That always bothered you, didn't it," Gail says softly.

"Yes," her husband replies. "I didn't think he took it to the limit. But we enjoyed the ride. I just wonder what he thinks when he sees Justin and Phil and Harrison Frazer out on the Tour. And I always wondered what made him go so bad. Was it his hands or his mind?"

. . .

Five days a week, Jeff Wolff walks through revolving doors into the polished, echoing lobby of JPMorgan Chase Tower. A high-speed elevator zips him to the twenty-eighth floor. He nods to the receptionist. Enters his office. Sits in a high-backed leather chair. Opens his briefcase – a case that actually contains briefs, the legal kind – and then it's down to work. He's an attorney at Fulbright & Jaworski, one of the top law firms in the world. Outside his window, downtown Dallas looks small and orderly.

At age thirty-four, Jeff reminds you of those Renaissance paintings that depicted children as miniature adults. He looks just like that kid in his scrapbooks, possibly because he was never so much a little child as a junior man. He's got his mother's bright blue eyes and an intense aura composed, I think, of intellect and wariness.

Away from the legal hush of the office, the grown-up prodigy opens up, but he's not a talker like his father. ("He's a defense attorney, but he doesn't go in the courtroom," Dr. Bill Wolff had said of his son. "He can't bullshit anybody.") I watch him play in the state amateur at Dallas Country Club. I meet his fiancée, the prettiest girl in Texas, Nikki Pierce. We eat lunch at a soup and sandwich place near his office. And we play eighteen holes and drink a beer or two at Dallas Athletic Club, his home course. He answers every question along the way, even on the unpleasant but unavoidable subject of failure.

"My dad is such a good athlete, but he didn't know anything about the golf swing," Jeff says, trying to keep crumbs from potato chips and the Number Six sub off his blue suit. "So when he saw how well I hit it, he never suggested the possibility of changing my grip."

Golf was never something they did together: "Once, when I was fifteen or sixteen, we played in the Father-Son at Colonial. We didn't do too well. He doesn't like to lose. We didn't do that again.

"It's amazing to me how supportive they were, and the sacrifices they made for me. We were gone three weeks every month in the summer. Luckily, dad had his own practice. Similar to what I do now."

Why did his game go south? "You start getting burnout issues," Jeff says, and by "you" he obviously means himself. "Who cares if you're good at age six? Age fifteen or sixteen is when it counts, and twenty-four or twenty-five is when it really counts. When you suddenly start getting beat, there's a lot of frustration. It wears on you mentally."

His frustration grew through his late teens until it boiled over at age twenty. He attended LSU on a scholarship, but college golf was more a trial than a joy. A big part of that was his severe case of the yips – "you get over a two-footer and don't even think you can hit the hole" – so he transferred his focus to his studies and got As, while his roommate, another golfer, rarely went to class. The coach encouraged him not to take any classes after one P.M. because the team practiced together in the afternoon, but Jeff couldn't always comply. The coach asked him to redshirt – that is, to sit out a year and work on his game, in hopes that he'd be a world-beater again as a fifth-year senior. Jeff said no. He worked hard on his game the summer before his junior year but when he returned to Baton Rouge in the fall, the coach told him there was no place on the team for him. His scholarship was revoked.

"It never was a ball striking issue," Jeff is saying. Just as his father had toyed with me on the tennis court, now his son makes my golf game look puny. His driver crashes into his Titleist Pro V1 the way a bowling ball crashes into pins. His tape-measure shot into the wind on the seventh hole on the Gold Course at Dallas Athletic Club goes 320. But then he has to putt. "I hate the guy who hits a three iron from one seventy-five and misses the green but gets it up and down for a four," he says. "And I hit driver-wedge and make six." And that is approximately what happens during our round. His unusual grip poses no handicap for full shots but his putter makes him mutter.

Yet there's a straight line between Jeff's jerky stroke and his graduation from LSU with honors, and cum laude from SMU Law, and his big job with Fulbright & Jaworski. If he'd stuck with golf, he'd probably be stuck with a Hooters waitress instead of planning a honeymoon with the lovely Nikki at the Four Seasons on Oahu. Is he happy? I don't know. He's not the easiest guy to read. No one who misses short putts is ever truly happy.

Before meeting the Wolffs, I'd assumed this paragraph from *Dr. Spock on Parenting* would be on point:

> When parents do sometimes succeed in pushing their children to excel in some field, such as ballet or music, the children may end up somewhat lopsided in development, perhaps self-centered or humorless or unsociable. They may also grow up feeling that their parents value them only for their unusual talent.

But that was not the case here. As his nativist method of holding onto a club proved, Jeff was a self-directed prodigy. His impulse to practice, his success, and his decline and fall were all or mostly *him,* not his dad. And those who believe that playing on the PGA Tour automatically makes you a successful person haven't spent enough time on the PGA Tour. So Jeff didn't really fail; in fact, the Wolffs are living a three-part happy ending, which sounds in my mind's ear like the xylophone tones on NBC TV.

Bing: Possibly because Jeff's retirement from single life allows him to answer his phone more often, he and his dad are talking more these days than in years.

Bong: For his last birthday, Jeff bought his dad a set of clubs – Ping irons and Cleveland woods, the same brands he plays. Jeff checked on the sticks during a recent visit home. "Dad," he teased. "They're still not dirty." A back injury suffered in a recent tennis tournament has Bill thinking about sports that don't tax his body so much. One day soon he and his son will play golf together again for the first time in a long time.

Bing: Jeff fell back in love with the game. "My dream is to play in the United States Amateur," he says.

"If we ever have kids, yes, I'd introduce them to golf. At minimum, it's great babysitting."

7

FAR

Erling, David, Peter, Paul, and Susan Jacobsen

The fat brown football hung in the cool autumn sky. Eleven Ducks held it in their gaze as they ran down the field, not an easy thing to do, because an equal number of Rams were attempting to knock the quackers on their asses and practically all the thousands of fans in the stadium wanted them to do exactly that. This was a home game for Fordham, at the Polo Grounds in the Bronx, New York City, Saturday afternoon, October 15, 1938. The Rams were beasts in the East; they had been undefeated in '37 and would drop only one game in '38. The boys from the University of Oregon, on the other hand, lost about as many as they won. But they looked vivid in their white jerseys with green numerals over emerald pants. The white pattern painted on their leather helmets resembled headphones or earmuffs. Fordham wore maroon.

above: The Jacobsen clan, from left: Susie, Peter, Erling, and David.

As the punted ball tumbled down from its apogee, its potential receiver extended his right arm and waved, a gesture indicating his wish to catch the thing unmolested in return for a promise to not advance after he caught it. But one running Duck, number forty-nine, missed or ignored the white flag, and he leveled the Fordham man with such extreme prejudice that spectators gasped before they started to boo. Referees immediately threw Erling Jacobsen out of the game.

Fordham won, 26-0. The momentarily disgraced football player boarded a train with his teammates for the long slow ride back to Oregon. He'd traveled from one coast to the other and back for a football game in which he lasted only four plays.

What manner of man would he become? The verdict among his friends and family fifty-odd years later would be surprisingly unanimous. Erling Eugene Jacobsen was a gentleman but not a gentle man, simultaneously fierce and funny, stoic and strict. A caddie as a kid, he held out golf to his wife and children as a suitable activity, and he guided the project along until their cumulative handicap was twenty-seven, a microscopic number for a family of six. Despite the most severe provocations, he never complained, and he couldn't tolerate those who did. He was a stickler regarding rules and comportment and had a complementary and frequently expressed disdain for golf carts and for the wimps who would ride in them. He taught his kids by the hour and they won tournaments by the score, but he almost never watched them in competition.

A moment: Erling came to breakfast dressed for work one morning and observed his two college-aged sons at the table digging into bowls of corn flakes. "What the hell are you doing here?" he asked. We're playing in the Oregon Open, they explained. It started yesterday. Father snapped open the sports page and observed a headline: JACOBSEN'S 68 LEADS OPEN. "Maybe you should withdraw and go back to Eugene," he said to the tournament leader, Peter, and to his oldest son, David, who'd shot a few more than his brother. "You boys need to focus on your studies."

"I knew Erling since the late forties," says Tom Edlefsen. "A character. Jesus. A firecracker. A very positive man but not flexible *at all;* there was no difference of opinion with him. He was tough with those kids. Tough love, although that was a term we never used. He insisted they do it right.

"He could be difficult as hell. When I was president of the club, he became unhappy with some trivial thing – a branch was trimmed incorrectly or something – so he asked me, 'Did you have anything to do with this?' And I said, I guess so, I'm the president. He said, 'Then you should resign.' He and his brother Leif, they were Vikings, believe me.

"He was a damn good man."

If you don't look too closely, the incidents and accidents around the gruff but benign patriarch seem like fodder for a television sitcom. His wife and golf tournament–winning kids loved him, and indulged him. Their conflicts could easily be portrayed as mild and comedic, set at the country club, and resolved in half an hour. "Wow," he said, observing his daughter on the practice tee once. "Someone's gained some weight." Consciousness-raising on what puberty does to girls' hips – that could be an episode. He was a prankster: while on vacation, he used breadcrumbs to lure a couple of geese into his sons' bedroom to wake them up. The birds accomplished their mission, but it was messy. He was a disciplinarian: when teenaged Peter threw a club and uttered several magic words that we'd have to bleep, Erling ordered him off the golf course. Peter couldn't wait in the clubhouse and have everyone ask him what was going on, so he sat in the car for an hour or two, muttering and alone with his thoughts. That's a show. And there'd be some laughs in this golf dad's wonderful lack of awareness of popular culture. Once he was invited to walk inside the ropes at a celebrity pro-am, the better to mingle with his son Peter and Clint Eastwood. "So, Clint," he said, shaking the actor's hand. "What do you do?"

But Erling's journey was far too complex for a sitcom, and although it was frequently fun, it wasn't really funny. Life eventually hit him with its very worst. He became the guy getting clobbered when all he wanted was a fair catch.

The short silver prop plane zoomed through smoke and boiling air. As anti-aircraft fire popped and pinged into its wings, the pilot felt an irresistible desire to fly higher above the guns on Truk or Okinawa or Formosa, but he couldn't get high and stay there, not if he wanted to do his job. The Curtiss SB2C Scout, a dive-bomber, crew of two, held a thousand-pound bomb in its fuselage and smaller bombs under each wing. Pilot in front, gunner-navigator in the rear, both encased in a clear eggshell that allowed them to see and be seen. The "Helldiver" had to get ridiculously low – about 1,200 feet – to be effective. Erling Eugene Jacobsen flew from, and landed on, a carrier called the USS *Intrepid.*

Lieutenant Jacobsen's home in the ocean had two nicknames:

the Fighting I, because of all the action it saw in the Pacific war, and the Evil I, for the horrific damage it sustained. Torpedoes and kamikazes crashed into it, killing men and disrupting its ability to function. Once the *Intrepid* got hit so badly that its sailors sewed spare sheets of canvas and bits of this and that to make a sail, for God's sake, so they could limp east for repairs a little faster. Erling and other Navy men played basketball on deck. They discussed the relative merits of the SB2C – "Son of a Bitch 2nd Class" – with the plane it replaced, the Douglass SBD Dauntless. Landing on a short deck in the dark . . . roller-coaster ascents and descents . . . the crappy hydraulics and electrical on the SB2C, and how firing its twenty-millimeter cannon shook the plane so badly that you couldn't read the instruments . . . his problems with sleepwalking . . . the time he broke his neck in a crash landing, and the resultant year in traction . . . an aircraft carrier with a sail . . . death. What stories Erling could tell!

He didn't tell them. The navy flyboy accepted the Navy Cross and the Distinguished Flying Cross – "extreme gallantry" and "heroism . . . extraordinary achievement," the citations read – and returned to Portland to marry Barbara Patterson, a pretty girl who liked to laugh as much as he liked to keep his mouth shut. To be sure, part of his warrior's reticence was genetic. "How can you tell an outgoing Norwegian?" jokes David Jacobsen. "When he talks, he looks at *your* shoes." Erling was Norsk through and through; his parents met on the immigrant ship from Oslo to Ellis Island. Marie, his *mor,* was from Bergen, and would never learn much English. His *far,* Julius, the son of a fisherman from a northern fishing village, would himself be a fisherman and a longshoreman in the port of Portland, Oregon. To add a bit to the family's finances during father's long absences with the tuna fleet, Erling caddied a little at Alderwood, a long-gone course near what is now Portland International Airport, and a lot at Riverside, where he won the caddie championship in 1929.

The milestones in his life are easily told: Jefferson High; a football scholarship to the U of O; a bit of pro football in Los Angeles in which he got a broken nose from a knee in the face; war; marriage. Four kids: David, Peter, Paul, and Susan. *Far* assigned the nicknames: Fobber (David's early attempt at "Father"), FB (Fat Butt), Pupper (Paul's favorite stuffed toy animal was a puppy), and Princess Bubbles. David and Paul resembled their father and inherited some of his reserved style. Peter and Susan replicated their mother's good looks and champagne-bubble personality.

Erling provided by selling insurance for the W. R. Reed Company, an odd choice for a quiet man. "He started as an administrator," recalls Peter Walsh, a close friend. "Sales was difficult for him, because he didn't have the ability to put himself in other people's shoes . . . I think he was troubled in his business life, and by some of his kids." But Erling – or Jake, as everyone called him – had the combat veteran's keen eye for what is important, what is trivial, and what is important trivia. Golf fit in the latter category. By three o'clock most weekdays, he had arrived at the practice tee at Waverley Country Club, a little slice of golf heaven in south Portland by the Willamette River.

Jake made golf the center of family life and put himself at the center of the golf. He kept it fun, and he made it more or less optional. "I'm going to the club," he'd say. "Anyone want to go?" If Erling's kids were going to play they were going to do it *right,* but the very idea of him insisting that one of them hit more practice balls causes David and Susie to smile and shake their heads.

On days they didn't have basketball practice, David and Peter took a city bus after school, transferred to another bus, hopped a fence, then walked along a railroad track to Waverley and dad. The Jacobsens built a green in their backyard, and evening putting competitions became a pleasant family ritual. ("David, the responsible one, did all the mowing and maintenance," recalls Susie. "Peter, Paul, and I would be inside, eating Reese's peanut butter cups and watching *Batman* on TV.") The word *vacation* meant golf vacation, usually at Astoria Country Club in Gearhart, a little coastal town up by the Washington border. Of the four kids, Paul was the only one not totally smitten with the game.

Which must have been a conflict: the Jacobsen children (except Paul) won tournaments right and left, and father evangelized with anyone who'd listen, especially new members, juniors, beginners, and the kids pushing greens mowers and raking bunkers. He preached for playing by the rules, and against golf carts and the concomitant evil of cart paths, which he believed defaced the playing surface. Beneath the vaulted ceiling in the living room, his kids swung clubs and he critiqued their action. His mantras on the practice tee and in the house were "Go back slow and turn your shoulders" and "Use your big muscles." Postround, his ritual questions were "Did you have fun?" and "What did you learn out there?" He believed in discipline; he did not believe in praise. "He'd never tell ya, 'nice going,'" Peter recalls.

"One of the big things he taught us was that life isn't always fair, and neither is golf," Susan says. "You can hit a perfect drive and your ball might hit a sprinkler head and go out of bounds."

When his kids achieved a certain level of competence with the playing part of the game, Erling stuck them in his weekend foursome, then watched them like a hawk for errors in manners or procedure, because there was way more to know than just the order of play. The Jacobsen children learned to listen attentively and respond appropriately as, for example, Mr. William Knight told still another story about his son Phil taking over the garage with all these molds and gadgets for making rubber soles for running shoes. (Phil Knight? You've heard of him – he started Nike.) Erling wound up with the most polite, pleasant young golfers around.

But: "I don't know how many times I played with him when he walked off the course," Walsh recalls. "He'd be bothered by a train whistle from twenty miles away, and the worse he played, the better his hearing. No, I wouldn't talk to him about it afterwards. That would have been like talking to your locker.

"A very complex personality . . . He could be real miserable. My degree in psychology is a little dusty, but I think he probably had an inferiority complex."

The Jacobsen kids never saw their dad not finish a round – "That would have been *completely* out of character for him," David says – and believe that Walsh's perspective is flavored by his feelings regarding the divorce. His wife was Barbara's best friend. As for an inferiority complex, Peter concedes the possibility: "He overcame a background that certainly was not silver-spoon."

But there could be no dispute regarding Erling's ability to

prepare and challenge golfers. Barbara, a beginner when she married, won the Waverley club championship. David, the oldest Jacobsen child, was, is, a hell of a player. He made the University of Oregon golf team, and qualified for the U.S. Amateur. He tried to qualify for the Tour a couple of times, and almost made it once. One year he reached the semifinals of the U.S. Mid-Amateur. Susan, a superb athlete, played in four national championships as a teenager and got to the semifinals of the Oregon Women's Amateur at age fifteen.

Peter outshone them all, of course. He made the Tour on his first try, and won big professional events and lots of money. Like his father, he was cool under pressure, and his bright personality – a gift from mom – attracted other stars, such as Jack Lemmon and Arnold Palmer. Like his friend Arnie, Peter had the very pleasing habit of granting respect to anyone he met, making strangers holding a Sharpie and a program feel they were at least as important as he was. The golf tournament he started, the Fred Meyer Challenge, raised millions for local charities. His Golden Tee video game became a staple of sports bars. He designed golf courses, he worked behind the mike for ABC TV for a year, he had a show on the Golf Channel, he formed and fronted a rock band called Jake Trout and the Flounders, and his golf clinic imitations of Arnie, Trevino, Craig Stadler, and Johnny Miller were the best sideshow on Tour. His two books – *Buried Lies* (1993) and *Embedded Balls* (2005), both written with former University of Oregon teammate Jack Sheehan – betrayed a nervous desire to entertain with joke after joke, but there was substance there, too, and *Lies* and *Balls* sold very well. Peter Jacobsen earned his success with hard work and handled it with grace.

His sibs had to adjust. They weren't just themselves anymore, they were . . . "We're very proud of Peter, and, really, the negatives have been so minimal," says Susan. "But I'm always introduced as 'Peter Jacobsen's sister,' as if I'm not smart enough or cute enough or funny enough to just be Susie. It's 'can you get me a book, can you get me a ticket, why did he miss that putt, can you get him to speak to our Rotary, and what does he think about Tiger?'"

As Peter's star rose higher, his younger brother receded from view.

Paul broke with the two main Jacobsen traditions. While golf preoccupied the rest of the family, Paul got down to an eight—good but far from great—then slowly drifted from the game. "No question—he didn't want to be out there [on the golf course]," says Peter Walsh. "He was *expected* to be out there." And he was expected to follow the path of his father, Uncle Leif, and brothers David and Peter to the University of Oregon and the Kappa Sigma house, but after high school Paul set off for the wilds of Los Angeles and Occidental College. He had to get away. He felt stifled.

"When Paul stopped playing golf, it was like permission for me to do something else," recalls Susan, the final Jacobsen to reach the post–high school crossroads. "It was, 'Oh, it's OK for me not to be interested in this.'" But Susan's disenchantment was a much bigger thing than Paul's. David thinks she had more talent and potential than anyone in the family, and lots of college golf coaches might have agreed. Among those offering scholarships were Arizona State, Oregon State, and—cue the fight song

—the University of Oregon. She turned them all down. Like Paul, she chose a little school in a big place over a big school in a little place, enrolling at Pitzer in Claremont, California, a liberal arts college thirty-five miles east of L.A. She played lacrosse, not golf, and had plenty of opportunities to hang with Paul, the sibling to whom she felt closest. Erling was not pleased with this turn of events—he nicknamed Susie's new school Armpit Normal—but what could he do? He had problems of his own. Barbara wanted a divorce.

A moment: bored with the drinking and small talk at his oldest son's July 1978 wedding reception—held, inevitably, at Waverley—Erling slipped out. The father of the groom walked to the golf shop in his good blue suit, got a club and a bucket of balls, and began caressing five iron shots out onto the soft green ground of the practice range, a former polo field. Barbara was furious. Ditching his own party was so . . . *Erling.* Soon after this incident, she moved out.

Person A in a family of six has a relationship with the other five, and those five have a unique interaction back to A. That's six times ten. Add the temporary alliances that form in any group and family mathematics can make you crazy. For a while, it seemed that Erling, David, and Peter were in one camp and Barbara, Paul, and Susan were in another. Everyone in the family felt pain from the split at the top, but the separation and divorce knocked Erling for a loop. He was devastated emotionally and horribly inept as a single man. For a solid year—the first year of the split—he ate dinner every night with David and his wife.

Then he got sick. There was some speculation that the cleaning solvents they used on board the *Intrepid* (or the USS *Enter-*

prise, the other carrier he served on) led to the cancer in his mouth. But once you've got it, the cause is moot; you've got to get rid of the active cells. Surgeons cut out most of his tongue. It seemed like one of those ironic punishments, like Monet going blind or Beethoven losing his hearing, because, on some topics, with some people, Erling could talk for hours.

Around this time, in the mid-to-late '80s, the problems of his youngest son came to a head. Peter wrote about it in *Buried Lies:*

> . . . there was a certain tension between Paul and the rest of the family that wouldn't go away. When Jan and I would go to Los Angeles each year for the L.A. Open, it seemed that Paul was usually too busy to come out to the course to watch me play. It was his way of telling me that his life was more important than coming to a golf tournament.
>
> About ten years ago, when Paul was twenty-six, he just blurted out something in a phone conversation with me. "You know I'm gay, don't you?" he said.
>
> I told him that of course I knew, and it was no big deal to me.

Paul was depressed, and he used a lot of cocaine and vodka, a horrid combination. But from rock bottom his life advanced in three giant steps: intervention, Betty Ford, and sobriety. "You've really come to a good place," David told him. "How did you do it?"

"I forgave myself," Paul replied.

Then acquired immune deficiency syndrome undid all his

progress, undid everything. Everyone in the family went to see Paul in his hospital room in Los Angeles, and everyone's heart broke when they saw how pale and thin their brother and son looked beneath the tangle of feeding and respiration tubes. And the fear in his eyes: "Peter, you can do anything," Paul wrote on a pad. "Please make this go away." He died a few days later. He was thirty-two. His death felt so intensely sad it was bizarre, David said.

Peter wrote that Paul's spirit had visited him at the exact moment of his death, at one-thirty in the morning, September 5, 1988. Barbara and the three surviving kids talked about their loss with those closest to them – Barbara had re-married – and with each other. But how would Erling, without a wife, or a publisher, or the ability to speak – express his grief? He spoke anyway.

They held Paul's memorial service at Trinity Episcopal Church in Portland. Susie felt surreal, not really in her body, as she eulogized her brother. She read something or other from Corinthians through tears that made it hard to see the page.

Erling's turn. He walked up eight wide, wooden steps to the carved white podium. He looked out into the vastness of the cathedral. Behind him, high above the altar, light shone through a circular, mostly blue, stained-glass window. The father spoke very slowly, making a tremendous effort to be understood. His theme was the New Testament parable of the prodigal son, who leaves, squanders his inheritance, but comes back, and all is forgiven.

The drive to Waverley from Lake Oswego looks a little like the opening sequence of *The Sopranos*. You cross the Willamette on the Sellwood Bridge and look through the concrete railing to see what ships and boats might be floating on the river, which is 75 feet below, and about 125 yards wide at this point. You pass through a mixed neighborhood, not urban New Jersey, but not very fancy – the Columbia Sportswear outlet store, Big Wong Chinese Buffet, modest houses and apartments, battered green Volvos that know the way to Mount Hood for snowboarding . . . right on Seventeenth. A diner, a place to get your oil changed in ten minutes. Another mile and the real estate becomes perceptibly more expensive. The small painted sign is on the right – the words *Waverley Country Club* appear in back-slanting cursive. Sun dapples the car windows – they have sunny days in Portland! – as you roll down the narrow winding driveway. Stone mansions partially obscured by tall hedges on the left and a lush green golf course on the right, and beyond the seventeenth and eighteenth fairways – we've traveled in a half-circle – the river. If you're lucky, you'll see a golf ball hit from the first tee hanging in the air, because that's a thrilling sight when you're in a moving car.

The first at Waverley is a short par four you should birdie every time but seldom do. From its tee, scratch men like David Jacobsen and Bucky Sheffield aim a two or three iron at the fir trees on the left, and cut it slightly, because you've got to keep the ball in the left third of the fairway and stop it at the top of the hill. Weaker players – me, for example – scrape out a five wood or a utility club. Erling, a lot shorter off the tee at the end, hit a driver.

Sheffield and Jacobsen Sr. played Waverley every Saturday at noon in any weather from July '87 until April '92. An odd couple: Bucky was a burly old boy (actually, young man) from Lubbock, a wheat trader with the gift of gab and a big golf game.

He'd played for Texas Tech. Erling was now a gray eminence with an ear-to-ear scar and a way of speaking that not everyone could get. "I spoke West Texan," Sheffield says. "I had no trouble understanding him." But the older man was losing weight, and though he still carried his clubs, he walked more slowly than before. He had relearned to swallow, eat, and talk, but cancer had returned, to his colon. It was killing him.

"I was away from my own father, and Erling was a great mentor, a real man's man," says Sheffield. "Tougher than nails. A war hero. An inspirational guy. He never complained about anything and hated people who did. One time I spun a ball off the sixth green and started moaning about it. He says, 'You've been playing here how many goddamned years, and you never noticed that this green slopes?'

"He never bragged about his sons' golf games but he would talk about what a good man David is. And he certainly defended them. I remember the time he saw Fred Stickle, the editor of the *Oregonian,* right after his paper had printed negative stories about Peter and David. Erling goes up to him and says, 'If you write one more bad story about my family, I'm gonna beat the shit out of you.'

"By that time, he was really sick, and weighed about 135 pounds. But still trying to play, and still wouldn't ride in a cart. Sometimes I'd carry his clubs up a hill. *That* would piss him off."

Susan was going through a divorce as the '90s began, so it seemed to make sense to go home and take care of her ailing father. Home: Erling didn't leave the original family house after the divorce; he loved his yard and neighbors only slightly less than he loved his kids and golf. "I asked myself, what is this, 'On

Golden Pond?'" Susan recalls. "Are we mad at each other?" They weren't, or weren't any longer. They talked, and cried a little bit. She found "the coolest old leather bomber jacket" in his closet but that relic didn't prompt a conversation about the war – nothing did. One day he requested a little wine for his feeding tube and Susan complied. "Maybe if I burp I can taste it," the patient said.

Peter took Erling with him to Japan, and included him in events like the one with Clint Eastwood. David and his wife visited Erling's house constantly, and Gay became her father-in-law's nurse. "We were friends," Gay says softly. "Once he slapped me on the butt and said 'So round, so firm, so fully packed.' The canned tuna commercial."

"My dad was totally, completely humbled by it all," David says. Near the end, he and Peter moved back into their old bedroom, sleeping in the extra-long twin beds there. "Dad and I talked for hours and became dear friends. I learned more about him and about myself than I ever could have if it had all been smooth sailing."

Everyone in the family noticed the new Erling. "I had been uneasy with both his parents at first," recalls Jan Davis Jacobsen, Peter's wife. "But then he made an abrupt change, completely an about-face, and in a very short time. I think it was from Barbara leaving him, not the cancer. There was this softening of the shell he'd always worn. He said to me, 'I didn't understand we had problems.' I said, 'You know, that may be the problem.'

"I remember once, when I was pregnant with Michael, feeling sick, and Peter was out of town. Erling called, and I mentioned I wasn't feeling very well. He was there in fifteen minutes, saying 'You go upstairs and lie down, I'll watch the girls.' I found out later that that was the day he'd been told he had cancer."

He died on a hot day. He'd played golf until two months before his death. Both his sons had adopted his involved parenting style. David and Gay's boy Matt plays golf for U of O.

Susan typed a few words on the old Royal in her father's house, and read them at the memorial service:

> My first vivid memory of my father's love was during the Columbus Day storm of 1962. If you've been to the house – imagine the power of the wind that day at the highest elevation in town. While Mom took my brothers down to the basement, Dad grabbed me and we climbed into the fireplace. He held me so close I could hardly breathe. I was just shy of four years old.
>
> At dark times of my life I want to be back there in the cinders during the storm of the century, unquestionably safe and protected in my father's arms . . .
>
> Dad gave me so much more than a great golf swing. I love him and I'll miss him.

At the reception after the service, a little old man named John Carney summoned a son of Erling to come sit close because he had a story to tell – the football story. Peter Jacobsen had never heard it before, and his eyes widened in amazement.

His dad had been such a tough son of a bitch. And such a nice man.

8

DON'T HIT THIS CLUB UNLESS YOU'VE GOT FIVE HUNDRED DOLLARS

Lee and Daniel Trevino

With the subtlety of a diplomat signaling a colleague for an off-the-record meeting, my father would nod at me and gesture with his eyes. Blue fumes from his pipe scented the air with the dark aroma of Amphora. "You have anything special at school tomorrow?" he'd ask in a voice my siblings could not hear. "Want to go to Firestone?" My answers were always no and yes.

Those were delicious days, watching four great golfers play a slow game of best ball in the CBS Golf Classic. The show was taped in the fall in Akron for broadcast on weekend winter afternoons. Retired rubber workers filled the small galleries – we two hooky players from work and school seemed always to be the only ones under age sixty-five. This led to a persistent waking dream, embarrassing to recall now: one of the four professionals would injure his hand or his elbow and be forced to drop out in

above: LEE TREVINO WITH HIS SON DANIEL.

the middle of the round. Consternation all around. The producer would scan the crowd for a likely substitute, and his eye would light on fourteen-year-old me. "You play golf, son?" Standing beneath a brilliantly colored oak or maple – perhaps a crimson leaf would flutter down – I'd demonstrate my flawless swing with an umbrella or a stick . . . The fantasy came complete with a story in the Akron *Beacon Journal:* "Local youth replaces Snead, birdies three holes to lead Dickinson to win in CBS golf action." Dad would look on approvingly, as applause and pipe smoke rose to the sky.

Finally, it happened. Someone became ill, and I was asked to fill in. But the injured – that is, severely hung-over – participant was a gentleman named Clarence, who carried the sign with the players' names and the match score. That day it was Miller Barber and Orville Moody versus Tommy Bolt and Lee Trevino. My pay was $20 plus lunch, the same deal Clarence got.

Barber had an eccentric swing and a fussy persona but made everything with his Otey Crisman putter. Moody wore monumental, country-singer sideburns and hit his driver like a god. After a horrid long iron shot on the final hole, temperamental Tommy Bolt got so mad he walked into the woods to scream through clenched teeth and to pummel a tree with his *god . . . damn . . .* two iron. But easily the most vivid actor in the drama was Trevino, the previously unknown man from Texas who'd won the U.S. Open three months before. Although he didn't play that well, and he and Bolt got hammered four and three, laughing Lee entertained everyone on the grounds. After his partner's hack on the fifteenth tee, Trevino looked at the ground and then into the camera. "How come our divots go in a circle?" he said, giggling, and the gallery roared. I was thrilled when he sat across a small table from me at lunch. Then I was mystified, because Trevino ate while staring at his plate, refusing to speak or be spoken to. He didn't seem like the same person I'd watched all morning.

After the meal, I picked up my sign and walked to the tenth tee. My silent luncheon companion was already there, doing standup like a Las Vegas comedian.

Forty years later, the jokes are still coming. Trevino is doing a clinic at D.A.'s Spring Creek Golf, the initials *D.A.* referring to touring professional/architect Donald Albert Weibring and the words *Spring Creek Golf* representing his driving range in Plano, Texas. About a hundred of us form a semicircle around the magnetic man. A microphone is clipped to his collar; you hear him through two big speakers that have been bolted onto ear-level platforms. "I'm sixty-seven," he says, "and I've got a forty-seven-year-old wife. I leave home to rest, boy." Young wife jokes are a staple of Trevino's comedy and some of us have heard this one before, but we all laugh. We gape as he bangs out perfect shot after perfect shot with his perfectly odd swing. Then we laugh again.

"He's the greatest player in the world," he says of another pro. Pause. "From the neck down."

With his homemade nine wood, Trevino hits a roundhouse hook within a yard of a flagstick stuck on the right edge of a target green – "you can't hide that hole from me" – and then he hits the mirror image of the same shot, a towering slice that nearly lands in the hole. "I'm a fader," he says. "Outside and reroute is what I do. I hate a hook. I can't find that ball. If I played a hook, I'd be as skinny as Chi Chi."

Who hit more practice balls, you or Hogan? a spectator asks. "I don't think Hogan hit more balls than I did because he drank the hard stuff and I only drank beer."

It's hot. Trevino's black shorts and short black socks highlight his thick, stubby legs – not that great a look for him, to be honest – but a pushed-back black hat accentuates his beautiful head of gray hair. His sombrero logo decorates his hat and shirt. He keeps moving, moving, alternating ad libs with lines from his mental joke file. He extends his gloved left hand, waving it back and forth quickly, his trademark gesture, indicating disagreement or opposition. Often he'll set up the opposition himself. "There's too many clubs," he says, punctuating each comment with the wave. "The worst thing that ever happened was the sixty-degree wedge . . . Graphite ruined the game . . . You don't swing like this. No. I want you to take a divot with that fairway wood."

Trevino's new driver is the greatest club ever made, he says, although it has the same canned-ham-on-a-stick look of any modern wood. He offers to let a spectator hit it – "but only if you've got five hundred dollars to spend. Cuz I guarantee if you hit it, you'll want to buy it."

The demonstration adjourns amidst applause and copious thank-yous from Weibring. "Did you folks notice," D.A. says into a hand microphone, "that he didn't mis-hit even one shot?" Another ovation. Trevino unhooks the mike from his collar and waves to his fans. He pauses on his way to the parking lot for hugs and handshakes with old friends. Cameras and grins flash.

Forty steps from his big black Chevy Suburban, someone with a pen and a notebook looms. Trevino keeps walking. "What can I do for you," he says. Somber, suddenly.

"Lee, I'd like to ask you about these men who were important in your life." I show him my list. The list reads: Joe, caddies, Greenwood, USMC, Salinas, Hogan. "It's for a book about fathers. Do you have five minutes?"

He doesn't. Has to pick up his son. Now.

"Could I meet you at Preston Trail sometime? Tomorrow, the next day, maybe next week?"

No, he says. The club wouldn't allow it.

A dubious assertion, as transparently untrue as "I only drank beer"; the men-only course in north Dallas is famous for its lack of rules. Members drive their carts right on the tees at the Trail, if they damn well want to, even, they say, onto the greens. Mickey Mantle played nine holes in the nude there once.

Now I know my mission is futile. One more try for the hell of it: "The senior tour's in Texas in a couple of weeks. How about if we just make an appointment to talk on Tuesday in San Antonio?"

I don't make appointments, Trevino says, opening the driver's side door. Just look me up when you're down there.

And then he's gone. A black Suburban with blackened windows: his car looks identical to the bulletproof vehicles the president rides in.

Fans didn't see it, but everyone in professional golf in the last third of the twentieth century observed the two startlingly distinct Trevinos. The moody brooder and the clown coexisted within him, and, as with every aspect of his personality, you wonder if his fatherlessness had anything to do with it.

Lee and his short, fat mother Juanita and his short, wiry

grandfather Joe lived in a shack. The unpainted building was part of the compensation package grandpa earned for digging graves with a pick and shovel. It had a dirt floor – at least in the kitchen – and no electricity, running water, or telephone. But it had acres to run around in, and a pond, and a close-up view of the seventh fairway of the Dallas Athletic Club golf course.

Joe taught Lee to work, harvesting cotton and planting onions – by hand, of course – and how to hunt rabbits and birds and crayfish. The Trevinos had a cow named Katie, a few hogs, and a big garden. Once, while fishing, a sudden hailstorm caught Joe and Lee in the open. They ran for the shelter of the family car, a '29 Model A, but the hailstones tore through the tar-and-fabric roof. Joe protected his grandson with his body, a moment Lee never forgot. He often walked the mile to the cemetery to deliver meat and tortillas for grandpa's lunch. Depending on where he was in the process, Joe could be hard to find. Lee admired the perfect symmetry of the holes he dug. Six feet deep, seven feet long, three feet wide.

"I have a faint memory of my mother once taking me to visit a man who may have been my father," Trevino told *Dallas Morning News* writer Sam Blair for their book *They Call Me Super Mex* (Random House, 1982). "We walked two or three miles through the snow and ice to this old house. We went in and there was this man propped up in bed.

"I didn't think that much about not knowing my father when I was a kid . . . It's not a sensitive subject with me . . . Besides, my grandfather was the best father I could have ever had."

At age eight, Lee wandered over to the nearby golf course. Soon he had a rough new set of friends: the men and boys in the caddie yard. Some carried knives and didn't mind fighting with them. Joe Trevino's influence waned, and his grandson changed. Something in the caddie milieu inspires gambling, comically overdone swearing, and self-consciously casual, cinematic cigarette smoking, and so it was at DAC. Schizophrenia, too: out on the course, the caddies were the soul of comportment, yes-sirring and no-sirring the golfers from whom they wanted a tip. Back behind the fence, they threatened each other like dogs in an overcrowded pen. Which is not to say that the caddie life cannot be fun. The DAC inmates set up three holes of 60, 100, and 125 yards, and a whole bunch of men and boys shared a couple of clubs for quarter-a-man, closest-to-the-pin contests. Picture the Texas heat and the heckling; Lee inventing a swing; and winning sometimes. He didn't go to school much and he didn't go at all after seventh grade. He was a happy kid.

Who was your daddy, Lee Trevino? Was it Hardy Greenwood? Greenwood had run a Japanese prisoner-of-war camp on Corregidor. Postwar, he leveled the ground on leased land near Greenville and Lovers in Dallas, put up lights and a building and a fence, and called it Hardy's Driving Range. It was just a couple of miles from the Trevino shack. The old pro noticed the strong brown kid the first time he came to hit. He was only eight? Funny stroke but man, he hit it so solidly and so far. After all those controlled shots he'd hit in the caddie yard, Lee enjoyed nothing more than whacking the hell out of a golf ball off a rubber tube with a borrowed driver at Hardy's.

"Greenwood was probably the strongest father figure he ever had," says Blair, Trevino's coauthor. Greenwood planted the idea in Lee's mind that he could make a living in the game. The older man cared about the boy enough to challenge him, and to hire him, and, when he screwed up, to fire him. Lee, lost, enlisted in the Marines. And when he came back four years later, Greenwood hired him again.

Thumbs down the seam of your trousers, palms in, eyes straight ahead, tattoos . . . the USMC taught Trevino how to stand and how to be one version of a man. That might be enough to have made the Marines at least a figurative father. And, like fathers of old, it gave him his profession. Due to a clerical error two and a half years into his service, a captain assigned Lee to Special Services, while all the other guys he'd been shipped to Okinawa with got Reconnaissance. Sweet! Trevino's assignment required him to issue socks and jocks, and to drive the football team to its games around the island – and to play golf almost every afternoon with officers.

Back in Dallas, the twenty-one-year-old Marine Corps veteran quickly accumulated a seventeen-year-old bride, Linda; and a son, Ricky. He ignored them, for the most part, in favor of golf. A few months after his divorce three years later, he tried again, with another seventeen-year-old, Claudia, and another child, Lesley. Hardy Greenwood opposed both marriages. When Lee felt competent enough for a try at the tour, Greenwood would not sign his application. "You're too immature to do this," the old pro said. Fresh in his mind was the $600 he'd given his protégé for a tournament in Louisiana, most of which Lee left on the bar in Lake Charles. "To hell with it," Trevino said. "I quit."

His ritual during these years, the early '60s, called for eighteen holes at dawn at city-owned Tenison Park, then the two-o'-clock-to-closing shift at the driving range. He met Arnold Salinas at Tenison – the best Mexican-American golfer in Dallas during Lee's time in the Corps – and they hit it off. As he spun out of Greenwood's orbit, Trevino embraced and was embraced by the seven Salinas siblings, and by their parents, Andrew and Angie. Lee eventually employed Arnold and his brother Albert as his agents. Blair recalls being with the clan at the Texas Open in San Antonio in 1979 or 1980, when "Lee called Andrew Salinas 'Daddy.' Affectionately, no put-on about it."

No one ever called the forbidding Ben Hogan "Daddy," but he was for Trevino a fatherlike ideal, a model for how to succeed and how to practice. And for how to hit a golf ball: when Lee got out of the Marines, he played a hook. The aggressive but hard to control right-to-left curve ceased being his basic shot the day he and Greenwood were invited to play Shady Oaks, Hogan's home course, because there on the practice tee was the Hawk himself, drilling out gentle fades to a caddie two hundred yards distant. Trevino dared not approach the great man, but he studied his flight path. And then, back at Hardy's, he hit about a million practice shots to groove a figure-eight-shaped swing that produced shots like the ones Hogan hit.

The two had a respectful but distant relationship over the years. When his equipment company tinkered with new designs, Hogan would order the prototypes sent to Trevino for testing. "Send them to the little Mexican kid in Dallas," he'd say, according to the often-repeated anecdote. "He hits the ball more solidly than anyone."

Who's your daddy, Lee Trevino? Who gave you love, who taught you how to be a man, who did you copy when you stopped being a mere sports star and started being a father? Over the years Trevino has occasionally spoken with me at such length I got writer's cramp taking notes, but he's not talking now, not about being a son and a dad. So I went to Orlando for the Del Webb Father/Son Challenge at ChampionsGate, a golf tournament in which the theme of this book is never far from anyone's thoughts. And everyone talks.

Time stretches like taffy for the security guard and me. He sits, I stand, in the shadow of a palm outside the players-their children-their agents-their caddies-their friends-only locker room at ChampionsGate Golf Club. It's quiet a few days before the competition starts – I'm the only one Officer Adam Smith has to keep out. We chat. He's twenty-seven, married, two children, works for the Osceola County Police Department, and the youngest person he's ever arrested was a nine-year-old who beat up his teacher. As if it's Career Day and I'm a second grader, Officer Smith agrees to identify the array of armament and accoutrement on his person: high-frequency radio; expandable baton; cayenne pepper spray; handcuffs; Glock .45 semiautomatic with a light scope mounted on the bottom of the barrel; two extra thirteen-bullet magazines; Kevlar vest; and a cell phone snug in the epaulet on his left shoulder. On his beige shirt, a badge, nametag, and Iraq pin. "December 2001 until March 2003," he says. "Port security."

Officer Smith's father works for the well-known local employer, Disney. Warren Smith composes and performs – percussion, mostly – for the Big Mouse's stage shows and movie soundtracks. "Growing up it was music, music, music, then golf and music," Adam Smith says. "A little less golf now that my brother and I can beat him. But we've never had one bad day on the golf course . . . the game made our relationship stronger, much stronger. No matter what happened, we could go play golf."

They're warming up for the pro-am on the other side of the clubhouse, with amateurs on one end of the broad practice tee and most of the sixteen pairs of fathers and sons on the other. There's Bob Charles and his son, David, hitting balls with their heads almost touching, because the British Open champion is a lefty and his identically tall offspring swings right-handed. There's Tom Kite, whose V-shaped torso reminds that he got religion on working out some years ago. He and his equally muscular son look like stevedores. Or Ph.D.'s in kinesiology: both Tom and David stop their swings at various stages of backswing and follow-through and examine their hands and arms as if searching for mites. The long, rhythmic swings of Vijay and Qass Singh are an aesthetic treat. Larry and Josh Nelson adjust their hats at the same time in the same way. Thomas Strange balances superbly during his stroke, just like his father, but Curtis is about to float off into the blue sky like a balloon, so great is his joy that his alma mater, Wake Forest, has made the Orange Bowl.

Arnold Palmer steps into the ring wearily, a fighter who has taken too many punches. Arnie, seventy-seven, once the most emotive man in sport, is subtle now. He has a chaste hug for Jennifer Mills, the brunette bombshell with USA Network, then he does his one millionth TV interview, then he takes some slow-motion swings next to his grandson, Sam Saunders. Sam's a big man and an excellent player – he won the USGA Junior a few years ago – and he bombs it with a precise upright stroke totally different from the *Mark of Zorro* slash grandpa used back in the day.

Now here comes Trevino, the prince of the tee if not the actual king. People gather in his wake as he walks along, as if they were water skiers and he were the boat. Heads turn, people stop hitting – even Hale Irwin, who has seen this pageant a few times – and the mood on the tee is suddenly lighter and more fun. The star is convulsed frequently by what people say to him as he signs autographs. He cracks them up, too; one of his humorous anecdotes ends with ". . . and I've got six kids!" Trevino decides to give a lesson, loudly – a lesson for everyone, really. He bustles up to a gray-haired amateur, a CEO, maybe, in a navy blue golf shirt. As the man starts his backswing, Trevino grabs the club – a classic, old-time teaching pro move. "No," he says. "No. I want that club back here, back inside" – he guides the man's club and his attached hands and arms – "cuz you can't do anything from out here. I want you to hit that ball at four o'clock, on the *inside.* Not out there at one and two.

"David Leadbetter doesn't know shit," he says, gesturing – his hand wave – toward the famous instructor's world headquarters at the opposite end of the range, a stucco building with an orange tile roof. This laughable assertion gets only nervous laughter. Did he really say that? "All Leadbetter wants to talk about is square: square shoulders, square stance, hit it square. No. You can't *get* to square if you're not a young man. You've got to open that stance and you've got to go inside your ball, not outside. You rotate from the inside. Never go on the outside of a ball."

Navy Shirt must be shocked at suddenly standing in the spotlight but he plays along, and tries one on his own. But his cautious swipe with his usual outside-in Ferris wheel results in a low, hard shot, an ugly thing.

"Here, try my driver," Trevino says. "But don't hit that club unless you want to spend five hundred dollars. Cuz you're gonna throw that old driver away." But the greatest club ever made produces no miracles in this man's hands, and, as the Trevino Show hits a lull, Lee turns his attention to his partner in the Del Webb Father/Son Challenge at ChampionsGate. Daniel Trevino is a handsome boy, barely fourteen, with a pale complexion and a geometrically cut mop of hair. He's small like his dad; otherwise, there's no family resemblance. Looks like his mother, who some call Claudia Two. Trevino had the one child with his first wife, Linda, who lived, except for a brief interval, with his mother in Missouri and Florida. Then three kids with Claudia the First—Lesley, Tony Lee, and Troy (a girl). Then, following some hair-raising public fights and a divorce, he hooked up with another Claudia, this one the daughter of a Connecticut golf pro. They had Olivia Leigh and Daniel Lee.

Single-mindedness made an absentee father of Trevino with his first set of kids, and success distanced him from the second. But he dotes on his third. He's encouraging and upbeat with Daniel. As his son warms up, the father peppers him with encouragement wrapped in discouragingly long sentences. As: "I want you to get your hands up, up here like this, cuz see, your hands are down here, because if you get 'em up, then you can rotate, like this, see? . . . Not enough rotation, more rotation, let it go . . . See, that's better."

Daniel has a beautiful, flowing swing, obviously the product of the excellent instructors at Preston Trail or Dallas National, the two clubs where his father belongs. Daniel's a rich kid, having a childhood 180 degrees from the one his father had. He and Olivia not only go to school, they go to the best private schools in Dallas. Their father's identity and love is never in doubt. Their home is grand, encompassing acres of expensive real estate near Inwood Road and Strait Lane. "It's a ten-dollar cab ride from your front gate to your house," Blair always jokes to his coauthor. Nearby and very far away are the cemetery where great-grandpa dug graves and the land once adorned by a golf course and a shack.

Late in the hot afternoon, by the locker-room door, Trevino again makes me feel like an insurance salesman. Officer Smith watches me get shot down like an enemy jet: um, I say, could we talk for a minute, Lee? "Not today," he says. How about tomorrow, before you play the practice round? You tee off at 10:20. Say, nine o'clock? "Not before I play," he says. "I never do interviews before I play." The next morning I watch as he does a TV interview before he plays.

I'd like to tell you about our whole life policies, Mr. Trevino, and then our term, auto, medical, dental, homeowners . . .

Trevino discussed his on/off switch in his autobiography:

> I give it a thousand percent when I'm out there. When I get out of that car at the course, I'm on stage. I'm the Muhammad Ali of the tour. Well, maybe I'm more than that. I've been with Muhammad Ali on a few occasions, on talk shows and such. You can sit with him backstage

and he never says a word. But as soon as he walks out and the camera goes on, he goes into his act . . . With me, it's no act.

I'm public property. I've created that by having a happy-go-lucky personality. But I can't stay open for business twenty-four hours a day. I need time for myself like any human being. That's why I've become a hermit on the road.

The entertainer personality may amuse but you don't need to be Dr. Phil to see how aggressive and controlling it is. The uncertainties of give-and-take are not on the table when one of us is performing. Why Trevino needs to control surely speaks to the out-of-control feelings he had from being from the wrong side of the tracks, and Mexican in a very white sport, and – maybe – from being fatherless. Perhaps he can't be figured out from this distance.

"I don't know if it's instinctive with him or serving a purpose," says Turk Pipken, the golf writer-filmmaker-comedian who once toured with Rodney Dangerfield. "I do know it's intimidating to gamble against a devil-may-care attitude. The perfect example with Lee is the snake at Merion, the hugest breach of decorum in golf history."

Historians will recall that Trevino and Nicklaus tied for first in the U.S. Open at Merion in June 1971. While waiting on the first tee before the playoff began, Trevino pulled a rubber snake from his bag and did some shtick and got big laughs from the crowd. Nicklaus played along but he desired levity at this moment about as much as he wanted to play in high heels. Although he never said so, Jack knew his opponent was screwing with him. Nothing similar to Trevino's prop comedy has occurred in golf's long history, before or since. Lee won the playoff, 68 to 71.

"A couple of times I played with Trevino and Willie (Nelson) at Pedernales, Willie's club," Pipken recalls. "Once, I had a six-footer for eagle to beat Lee's birdie. I take a couple of practice strokes and Lee says 'No, no, Hoss, you'll never make it like that' and he proceeds to give me a three-minute putting lesson. I missed the putt, of course. There's a huge ego there, and he's very competitive.

"As for his personality when he's not performing – look, you have to get up to get on stage, and it's natural to come down. Rodney's 'I don't get no respect' act was true in a way that wasn't funny offstage. People were always amazed when they met him that he didn't make them laugh."

Although Trevino seems uninterested in discussing the subject, other famous men on the practice tee are happy to think out loud about golf and dads.

Like Lee, Curtis Strange won two U.S. Opens, and he too lost his father. He pauses between practice shots, feeling the life-affirming glow of Florida sun and Wake Forest's winning football team. "I loved every minute of it," he says of a youth spent on a golf course where his father was the pro and owner. But dad was no rainy-day philosophizer, gassing on with advice and parables for his son. He taught by example, keeping a little distance from, and granting independence to, Curtis and his twin brother, Allen. In the summer of '69, after a short illness, Mr. Strange died of lung cancer. Curtis was fourteen when his father died. "I don't think you know what to think at that age," he recalls. "It's a cliché, I know, but my Dad would have wanted me to play. So I went back to what I knew, which was golf."

So when he had sons of his own, did he stand back like his dad, or did he try to groom the next Open champ? "He used to duct tape a club to our hands," says Tom Strange.

"Maybe the tape should have been over your mouth," replies his father.

No, says Tom, twenty-four, smiling now. All his father ever really insisted on was that he and his brother David get their asses outside when the sun was shining: "He didn't care what it was, building forts or playing games. When I was ten or twelve, golf wasn't cool. Then at age fifteen or sixteen, my friends started to play, so I did, too."

Tom played college golf at James Madison and North Carolina State. His father encouraged him, yet gave him space. "Especially this time of year, when I'm grinding to get ready for this tournament, it gets to the point where he won't tell me anything about my swing. 'Just keep doing what you're doing,' he says.

"With my last name, people expected me to play well. When I didn't, I was embarrassed. I didn't want people to know my name. They'd ask, 'Are you related to *that* Strange?' But being embarrassed was just pressure I put on myself. I'd say, 'Yes, that Strange.' My dad has such a good reputation. He was once the best there was. What son wouldn't be proud of him?"

Drew Nelson, son of Larry, is hitting drivers nearby, and smiting the ball so hard the earth shakes. He has the same deep shoulder turn as his father and a similarly retreating hairline. "We didn't know Dad was famous. He was just Dad," says Drew, wiping the sweat from his face. "When he won the U.S. Open in

'83, my brother and I didn't even watch it on TV. We were playing Frogger."

Drew and Josh grew up within one hundred yards of the practice tee at the Atlanta Athletic Club, but baseball and soccer held more fascination. And Drew and Josh held more fascination for Larry than golf. During his prime, when he won the U.S. Open and the PGA Championship twice, Nelson eschewed numerous events for guaranteed appearance money and strictly limited his time on the road. He had bigger fish to fry: coaching his sons in soccer, picking them up from school. Dad stuff. "I wouldn't trade those times for anything," Nelson says.

"I was aware he was taking time for us," says Josh, twenty-eight. "I never felt golf was more important than we were. He's such a great competitor – just look at his Ryder Cup record! He could have had a much bigger career if he'd played more."

Golf finally lured the boys to the practice tee. Drew stayed a little longer. He won the state high school championship, turned pro, enjoyed some success on various mini-tours, and almost made the PGA Tour until elbow injuries slowed his progress. Did his dad encourage him? "He's encouraged me to quit," Drew says. "I don't think it was ever his dream for me to play. His dream is for the three of us to work in a business together.

"People not in golf want the big career for their kids. People in golf know how hard it is. I don't want either of my kids to do this."

Are you related to *that* Trevino? Daniel will draw plenty of attention if he gets serious about his father's game. Yet despite his presence here and his obvious competence – not to mention his father's intense teaching style – that's not a sure thing. Daniel has never teed it up in an American Junior Golf Association event or in the junior tournaments run by the North Texas PGA. Perhaps Lee wants to make competitive golf available for his son without insisting on it. Maybe he's saving him.

The Trevinos have returned to the clubhouse after their practice round, and are putting gloves and tees into their matching golf bags – black, with their names in block letters below the sombrero logo – and taking keys and wallets out. I know he won't talk, but – how about a picture? And to this, Trevino immediately agrees. They stand very close to each other and the smiles are real.

9

OUR FATHER

Jack Burke Senior and Jack Burke Junior

Jack Burke's thoughts about golf and God arrive from heaven fully formed, with clauses and subclauses and bullet points. They go from brain to page in longhand, and thence to a hidey-hole – a leather binder, a wooden box, a bottom drawer – to be examined later under lamplight in his big dark office. If time has not damaged his aphorisms and predictions, they are added to his impressive verbal arsenal. He won the Masters, and the PGA Championship, and four tournaments in a row once, but this man is a speaker most of all.

No. "Speaker" doesn't do justice to his rhetorical style. No mere speaker gets in your face and in your mind like John Joseph Burke Junior. He handed Arnold Palmer a piece of nylon cord at the Champions Dinner at the 2006 Masters. What's this?

above: JOHN JOSEPH "JACK" BURKE SR. TEACHES HIS SON JACK JR.

Arnie asked. "It's a gallery rope," Burke replied. "You should get your [self] on the other side of it." Ouch! A touring pro came to him for a putting lesson, missed the first putt he tried from four feet, and seemed vaguely disappointed. Oh, darn . . . Burke startled the young man with a sharp rap on the noggin. "I want you to feel *pain* when you miss a putt!" he said. Another pro who had qualified for the Tour felt anxious about it, so he journeyed to Houston to ask the master for advice. They spoke on the patio on the golf-course side of the Champions Golf Club clubhouse. What should I expect? What should I look out for? the pro asked. Burke considered his answer while maneuvering the newbie to the edge of the concrete pad, six inches or so above the ground. Suddenly, the old man struck the young man hard on the shoulder, and Hal Sutton lost his balance. "About like that," Burke said. "Falling. Out of control . . ." But he caught his young friend before he fell.

A prop, a rap, a push, a catch . . . You've got to be ready for the sheer physicality of an interview with the owner-operator of Champions. It goes something like this, at least for me: "Hello, Mr. Burke," I say, entering his windowless office in the center of the clubhouse. As we shake hands, he uses his off-hand to poke me here and there on the torso, a gesture I'd resent from anyone else. "Pretty good," he says. But he doesn't like the way my arms hang from my shoulders, or how my thumbs attach to my hands . . . Apropos of physical fitness, he pulls a chair into the center of the room and holds it while he extends one leg, then the other, demonstrating aspects of his martial arts–based workout (he's got a black belt in tae kwon do). While I hold a persimmon driver plucked from a bag by his desk, he kneads my hands into a good grip, as if he's working with dough. Except for the lunch interval – he has half a cheese sandwich and a glass of tea – he won't sit during our hours together.

Left alone in his wood-paneled office for a few moments, I stare at framed photos of Hogan and other stars of an earlier era, then pull a couple of Burke's letters to himself from the middle of a tall stack. "The Future," reads one, written, apparently, in the early '60s. "Smaller clubhouse. No carts. Smaller set of clubs. Small enough bag to bring caddies back to the game." OK, he missed on that one – so far. Another missive mulls the meaning of the Catholic Mass. "You cannot give anything to God," it reads in part. "He doesn't need it. Every ticking second of the clock he is giving you life. Adore him, yes, honor him, yes, but don't try to give him anything."

The whirlwind returns. "The *church* was the first club," Burke says, grabbing a pen (mine) and a pad (his) to draw a series of boxes and squiggly lines, illustrating a premise he didn't just think of. "The farmers from here, here, here, hired a preacher to read the Bible to them. Afterward, they had lunch under the big oak tree. Someone says, 'Bring me a wagon part next Sunday.' They had a like interest – farming. They had a club.

"Now, we have a mute society. People join a golf club or tennis club but their jobs are so diverse they have no common interest. We're just lost."

Burke hands back the pen, taking the opportunity to palpate his guest's wrists and fingers. "Too stiff. Feel mine. Make a fist. See the way your thumb goes under there? You should set up to hit a golf ball like a boxer sets up to throw a punch."

As we fill my notebook for the next four hours, and as I drive home for four hours after that, a question buzzes like a fly from window to window inside my Toyota: If golf itself was a child, who would its father be? Our mythical patriarch would have to be a national figure, with authority derived from a distinguished career in the game. Most of us would reflexively nominate Arnie, because forty years after his prime as a player, he is still among the most popular sportsmen on the planet. But being Arnold Palmer is a full-time job, always has been, with demands to be nice and to sell hearing aids and motor oil that preclude a father's stewardship. Jack? With his five kids, several of whom work in the family golf-course-design business, Nicklaus is a very considerable golf dad. His is an important voice in the fight between golf and golf equipment manufacturers, and his transcendent skill has thrilled millions. But the father symbol of this particular sport would have to love teaching, and Nicklaus is not wired that way.

A beloved instructor of a certain age might be considered the Father of Modern Golf except that we children admire achievement more than wisdom, and it's hard to think of an important instructor with battlefield ribbons. That's not the way it works. Great players in their dotage go into the broadcast booth (Byron Nelson, Johnny Miller, Nick Faldo); they design golf courses (Nicklaus, Ben Crenshaw); they become pitchmen (Palmer); or they stay inside the endless cycle of country clubs and hotel rooms on the senior, AKA "Champions" Tour (Trevino, Tom Watson, Hale Irwin, and Palmer, again, until he just couldn't). They write instruction books or have them written for them but no one wins the Masters and *teaches.* Because teaching requires deep thinking and creativity, which is a different skill set from driving and chipping and putting, and it's hard work. And, relative to those other things, it's usually not that profitable.

There is, of course, the one unique man, the one I've just left, who won the Masters and the PGA and the Vardon Trophy and four tournaments in a row and then quit to get even *deeper* into the game, by building, owning, and operating his own golf club. His reputation as an instructor compels the likes of Phil Mickelson, Sutton, and Steve Elkington to go to him for help. They leave with something more than smoother putting strokes or tighter backswings or more organized thinking. After participating in one of Burke's forums on health, religion, politics, family —and, almost parenthetically, golf—these men with perfectly good fathers have all come to think of Burke as their golf daddy. Who else could humble the Everest-like egos of Phil and Steve? No one. Without question, Jack Burke Junior would make the best golf dad. He says what needs to be said whether we want to hear it or not. He is unique, sui generis.

Except that he's not. His father did it all first.

The humility and strength of Burke's origins is contained in the word *hod.*

A hod is a three-sided wooden box on a long pole, used to hold bricks and mortar. The hod carrier climbs ladders and scaffolds with his heavy, awkward load balanced against his shoulder, delivering his goods to the masons above. The job requires balance and brawn and, by the end of the day, a willingness to suffer.

John Joseph Burke hoisted hods in Cork and carried them again when he migrated to Philadelphia from Ireland around the time of the American Civil War (his famous grandson is thus a

III, though he's never used the numerals and is always referred to as Junior). Philadelphia had plenty of work, and plenty of other Irish, and with its wooded hills and its great river, the city might have made Burke remember rural southern Ireland, at least a little. The Burkes had five kids: John Joseph Junior, Edmund, Mary, Winnifred, and Tom. They lived in a red brick house no architect would claim, a three-story box at 3692 Stanton, a steeply sloping street in an unpretentious section called Schuylkill Falls, now referred to as East Falls. The houses had flat roofs with drainpipes hung artlessly down exterior walls. Narrow alleys defined a line between every other dwelling. The Ivy Line train rumbled along the top of the hill. Two blocks down the hill the Schuylkill flowed silently past.

Hard-working gentlemen at their leisure drank beer and ate catfish and waffles at the Falls Tavern, an old whitewashed plaster building hard by the river. Many of the men toiled within walking distance of their homes – at the chemical plant, which vented horrid-smelling gases from the manufacture of quinine, or at Dobson Mills, whose contract to supply the Union side with army blankets kept it humming. Sunday meant a short walk up the hill to Saint Bridget's Roman Catholic Church. Afterward, after lunch, if the weather was nice, families liked to sit on the banks of the Schuylkill and watch the boats, and to roll up pant legs or hold up dresses and dangle their ivory white feet in the warm brown water.

You could live your entire life in this neighborhood. Saint Bridget's opened a school in 1888 and the Sisters of Saint Joseph nuns were its teachers. The hod carrier's son, born the same year as the school, attended.

When not in school, kids worked. In those days before child labor laws, Dobson Mills offered minors employment from six A.M. to five P.M. and paid $3 for the week. Little Jack began to earn his keep at age nine, but not in the claustrophobic, ear-splitting din of a knitting mill. He walked uphill three-quarters of a mile and entered the much more benign atmosphere at Philadelphia Country Club. He was a caddie, of course. Did the green grass and gentle contours of the ground remind him of Ireland, a place he'd never seen? Was he intrigued by the ball in the air, or by the men whose bags he carried, or by how one golfer seemed competent while this other one was awful? Perhaps the most important aspect of the experience was the subordinate role of the caddie. In order to actually play the fascinating game, Jack saw that he would have to earn his way in. He'd either have to become wealthy enough to join a club, or know so much about golf that he could teach it to others. The contrast to the modern approach is striking. Nowadays, the accent is on giving, not earning: *giving* underprivileged children access to golf, its rules, and its social benefits – as if golf were just another child's game, like basketball, and a birthright. But the caddie system worked damn well, while the jury is out on programs like The First Tee, and it may stay out forever.

Whatever: Jack Burke was hooked. The game put such a powerful spell on the boy that when he got his first club, he often slept with it. It had a hickory shaft, which wouldn't have been as cold at night as steel.

A handsome kid with high-thread-count black curly hair, Jack quickly achieved his adult height of five feet six and three-quarter inches. Short legs supporting a wide, strong torso gave him balance and power, and years in the caddie yard instilled a love for the looper's favorite pastime, gambling. He played quarterback in football and often swam in the Schuylkill but usually his hands were busy building clubs or hitting balls. He turned pro after completing high school and, as his skill and reputation grew, moved from this job to that for a few dollars more. His first posting was at Hershey Country Club, near Harrisburg, just ninety miles up the road. Then back home, to Aronimink Golf Club; thence to Hyperion Field Club, near Des Moines, in 1910 and 1911; Thunder Bay Country Club, on Lake Superior, north of Duluth; then a couple of gigs in suburban Chicago. Three stops in Texas – two in Fort Worth and one in San Antonio. Finally he landed, for good, more or less, at Town and Country Club in St. Paul. He wintered in Fort Worth, to teach at River Crest, where his brother Tom was the pro. And in Fort Worth he met the magnificently named Quo Vadis Quayle, and married her. They would have beautiful children – eight of them, seven of whom survived.

Quo Vadis had married the perfect pro. Jack Burke could teach, build and repair clubs, and grow grass – he'd been the pro/super several times, like Old Tom Morris. He communicated his thoughts with crystal clarity, and he comported himself like a gentleman. Above all, he could play the game as well as almost anyone, and his wins in various state opens filled his employers' hearts with pride. He was a regional star who went national at the U.S. Open at Inverness in Toledo in 1920.

> Enthusiasm was wild in the little suburb by Fairmount Park last night. Jack's great score was placed in the

> windows and rooms of every restaurant and store . . . They looked with awe at his grand total of 296, just the slender margin of one stroke behind Edward Ray, of Oxhey, England, and remarked happily that "Jack was the only Philadelphian to come through." (*The Philadelphia Enquirer,* August 14, 1920)

Obviously, they still remembered Jack back in Philly. In this same story, the *Enquirer* contacted Edward Clarey, a well-known local amateur, for his thoughts on the man of the hour. A rather breezy chap was Mr. Clarey, apparently:

> Jack's great ability, to my mind, lies in his willingness to take chances while playing. Sometimes the shots are called queer from the very nerve it requires to make them and the big chance involved, but "Smiling Jack" never hesitates . . . Outranking everything else, however, is Jack's gameness. Personally, I regard him as the best golf fighter on the links and he never really starts until he is down, then he plays sensationally.

Burke won $187.50 for his great finish, good money, but great money shimmered on the horizon. Now a pro people had heard of, a publisher in Saint Paul convinced him to write a book. *Ten Lessons with Jack Burke* is a little dated now but it had pith. In putting, Burke wrote, "the feet should be kept well together with the heels touching and the toes pointing outward at a slight angle. The weight of the body should be thrown a trifle to the right foot."

When the runner-up in the Open came to Houston to play in an invitational tournament at Houston Country Club, several gentlemen took pains to get to know him. A group led by the Hogg brothers, Will and Mike, sons of the former governor of Texas, had money like other people had socks – lots of it, in other words – and they were forming a development called River Oaks, which they planned to make the best neighborhood in Houston. A golf course would occupy the center of the thing, designed by the best architect in the world, Donald Ross. Now they wanted the best pro they could find. In an era when both Irish and golf professionals were an underclass, a man who was both stood out for his dignity and class. Burke.

Picture for a moment the poor but honest golf instructor in his plus fours coming home at the end of a weary day to his wife and kids to share a meal that wasn't prime rib and to get up to do it all again the next day. Now forget it: Burke usually wore pants, and River Oaks didn't do things cheaply. They paid their new man a salary of $45,000, a fortune in 1925. The Burkes had a maid – she cost $8 a week – and Jack suddenly had options he'd scarcely dreamed of. What if he owned his *own* golf course?

His oil millionaire members put the thought in his head. Impulsive men who'd gotten rich quick, their money couldn't disguise their lack of history in the game. Burke had spent most of his life with relatively learned patrons of golf at clubs in the north and east. But these Texans didn't know what they were doing and didn't appreciate what they had. Their insensitivity to the subtleties of Donald Ross's design annoyed their purist pro/superintendent, who had to listen when they asked him to fill in bunkers they'd found inconvenient and to remove trees that interfered with their slices. It made Burke imagine a club without time-wasting, authority-diffusing member committees, where no dilettante had any power over anything. Perhaps he talked about his idea with guests at his dinner table at home. At any rate, when Colonial Country Club – later called Brae Burn – became available in 1926, Burke and three other pros with good credit bought it. Course, clubhouse, and all cost $65,000. The timing seemed right, with the '20s roaring and golf booming. But after Black Friday came in October 1929, the $3,000 monthly payment overwhelmed the partners and their dream of golf pros leading a golf club died. So Burke remained at River Oaks, very often on the practice tee, usually with his little son Jackie by his side.

Jackie – Jack Junior – was a little kid with a big problem: he couldn't breathe. Until he was about twelve years old, almost any exertion might cause his lungs to spasm and then he'd be on his hands and knees, gasping. So while his father taught, Jackie sat on the ground or on the end of a golf bag, watching and listening. To help the novice who was hypnotized by the ball, Burke Senior would hide the pill under a leaf and tell the student to hit the leaf. He had a dozen tricks like that. "It's a simple game, and I'll teach it to you simply," the instructor would say. "There's a swing in everybody. We've just got to find your swing."

Some days, Jackie's most significant exercise came on that practice tee. To treat golf's most common malady, the slice, Burke Senior would have a student swing to the top, start down, then literally throw his club out on the range, hopefully conveying the feeling of releasing the hands at impact. Students would pitch out their entire set, and Jackie would pick them up. If they still hit a big curve ball, the pro would have them throw the clubs again.

Beginning at age three, Jackie spent day after day around the golf shop, on the golf course, in the bag room, on the practice tee, and, eventually—when his asthma started to clear up—in the caddie yard. Evenings were usually devoted to . . . more golf. "Where do you *find* these people?" Quo Vadis would whisper to her husband. Arrayed around her long rectangular dinner table, interspersed with Burke children—Jackie, Eddie, Catherine, Beverly, Billy, Jimmy, and Susanna—sat a changing cast of assistant pros, head professionals, and itinerant equipment salesmen. The River Oaks caddie-turned-assistant pro Jimmy Demaret was a regular, and the Burkes' regular babysitter. There was Jack Grout, Levi Lynch, Henry Picard, Johnny Dawson, a guy from East Texas remembered only as Clark, a pro from San Antonio named Tod Menefee, and quiet, bespectacled Harvey Penick, who wrote everything down in a little red notebook. (Demaret would win the Masters three times, and cofound Champions Golf Club with Junior; Grout would teach Jack Nicklaus; Picard won the Masters and the PGA Championship; Penick taught Kite and Crenshaw, then he taught everyone with *The Little Red Book,* a lot of which was taken verbatim from the Burke table.) "Get upstairs and do your homework," Quo Vadis would say to her starstruck son. "Stop listening to these golf pros." Burke Senior sat at the head of the table and directed the discussion on how to teach and how to play and who will win the U.S. Open. After the children had been excused, the men would refill their glasses with beer and get out the cards. They played Pitch. Money changed hands.

Gambling, little Jackie noticed, was absolutely vital in his father's world. There were pool tables in the locker rooms at River Oaks and the other clubs he visited, not so much for pool, but for dice. His dad loved to take the short trip south to Galveston, to try his luck in the casinos. "He's probably had a bet with most of his friends," wrote Clark Nealon in a profile in the *Houston Post*. "Jack'll back up his judgment or his golf game on anything from the toss of a coin to one of those jumpy little pitch shots he fires." Everyone at River Oaks considered a game of golf without a wager to be a hollow thing, as pointless as not keeping score. When a group of members lacked a quorum on the first tee, they'd often send word to the golf shop for the pro's kid to grab his clubs. Almost from the cradle, Jackie played for stakes. It made him like ice under pressure: he qualified for the U.S. Open at age eighteen. And at the Masters in '56, while a thirty-mile-an-hour wind made his pants flap like a flag on a pole, he stood over a four-footer to win. The gale had dehydrated the green and turned it to marble. With his feet kept well together, with the heels touching and the toes pointing outward at a slight angle, he made the putt.

Family, golf, gambling, and the Catholic Church were the cornerstones of this life. Jackie went to Saint Thomas High School and absorbed – permanently – the lessons and philosophies of the Basilian Fathers who taught there. When Grandpa came down from Philadelphia for visits that could last six months, he went to the early mass at Saint Anne's every day and took his grandson with him. Part of the old Irishman's ritual – it almost seemed like part of Communion – was a stop at a bar on the way home for one glass of beer.

Freud observed that children need their parents to die twice, but Jackie did not seem to require his father's symbolic death in order to assert his independence. He followed in Senior's footsteps very explicitly when he became a head professional at Galveston Country Club at age nineteen. He continued to look up to his dad, and to spend time with him whenever he could. Until he couldn't: Jackie enlisted in the Marines and shipped out to train to fight in the Pacific War. Father embraced son at the train station, then returned to work, and to work on a new book, in which the natural motions in other sports – firing a rifle, rolling a bowling ball, hitting a baseball – would be applied to golf.

But Jack Burke Senior never wrote that book, and he never saw his son again.

Seven hundred hard, sunburned men mustered at the hospital at Camp Pendleton, headquarters of the 1st Marine Division. After four months of intense, almost brutal training in weapons, war-craft, and physical fitness, assignments were being given. Smith got ordnance on the USS *Intrepid* while Jones would be Infantry on the *Enterprise.* A fraught atmosphere: war and all war implies was about to begin for the seven hundred.

"Burke, John Joseph!" a man with the clipboard shouted. "Fall out!" Burke, John Joseph was instructed to get in that truck over there, return to his barracks to change into dress khakis, and report to Colonel Ritterhoff. *Colonel?* In his brief military career, Burke had never even seen a rank higher than corporal. And why had he been singled out? Dazed and confused about what all this meant, the young Marine stood at attention in the Colonel's office.

"Your father write this?" Ritterhofff asked. He held up a copy of *Ten Lessons with Jack Burke.*

Yes, sir.

"Damn good book. And I understand you're a pro, too. I want you to build me a driving range. You can requisition materials as you need them. Start by making a list . . ." *What?* Private Burke quickly realized he would not be landing on a beach, firing his weapon and being fired upon. His feelings were mixed, to put it mildly. His sense of duty and loyalty to the men he'd trained with clashed with the simple fact that he probably would not be killed.

After putting together the tees and fences needed for the driving range, Burke spent the rest of the war as a drill instructor. Men had to know they could survive a jump off the deck of an aircraft carrier, so everyone had to step off a platform seventy feet in the air and go feet first into the pool below. Burke explained the correct way to hold your body in flight, and how to enter the water. Some men froze. Burke grabbed them and jumped with them. Aviators had to be taught how to survive on a tropical island if they were shot down. The young Marine marched them thirty-four miles to the coast and back, showing them the kill-or-be-killed tactics of hand-to-hand combat, how to read the silk maps they tucked in their survival kits, how to find water.

Burke and a sailor named Sam Snead occasionally spent entire days giving golf lessons to wounded veterans on the grounds at the Naval Hospital. From time to time Burke heard his father's words come out of his own mouth as he showed injured men how to grip a club or the correct mechanics for a bunker shot. He was his father's son.

Jack Burke Senior died suddenly – heart attack – in February 1943. He was fifty-four. Jackie rattled along on the train back to Houston for the funeral, thinking about his father for a thousand miles. His dad had been scheduled to play a war-bond charity match at River Oaks with Demaret, Byron Nelson, and Jug McSpaden. Jackie filled in for his father, and shot a 69 that beat the other three.

"We've got to get the amateur back," Jack Burke Junior says. We're in his office, in the twenty-first century, and so much has happened. "The amateur didn't return to the game after World War II, the developer did. Amateurs have to be the foundation. Not professionals. I don't think Corey Pavin and Jim Furyk are going to carry the game, do you?"

The light from ten huge windows infuses the clubhouse. You eat a Champions salad while observing the purposeful play on the putting green, and the first and tenth tees, and it all looks huge and cinematic, as if these eight-by-eight-foot sheets of glass are screens showing a never-ending golf movie. The food is good but it's not the point. At this club, it's golf, first, last, and always. "I don't think anyone should genuflect when the chef walks by," Burke says.

Burke is in his eighties now, but as he has all his life, he looks 20 percent younger than his years. Although his activity level has hardly abated – "I don't think reading the newspaper should be the highlight of your day," he says – he looks back at all those years from time to time. He has to, when once a week another writer wants to know about his seventeen wins or his five Ryder Cups or what Hogan was like. Perceiving a market for the irreverent way Burke expresses his reverence for the game, Gotham Books threw six figures at him in 2005. The result is *It's Only a Game: Words of Wisdom from a Lifetime in Golf.* It is, and they are. With its humor and its let's-cut-the-nonsense tone, *It's Only a Game* is the perfect accompaniment to *The Natural Way to Better Golf,* Burke's first book (Hanover House, 1954). His dedication in *The Natural Way* reads: "To my father, JACK BURKE, Sr."

"Most of Dad's truisms hold up today," Burke wrote in *It's Only a Game.* "Some of the others I disagree with. I idolized my father, but I suppose I've put in enough hours teaching over the years to disagree with him." In the book, he lists twenty-nine pearls of wisdom from his father, such as "try holding the right shoulder back as long as possible, [to] give the left side a chance to get through." Burke Junior endorses twenty-two of the twenty-nine, including that one.

They also agreed on much deeper things, of course, such as large families (Burke Junior has six kids), teaching, playing, course ownership, and applying an idealism to the game that is almost religious.

"You knew the parameters with my dad," Burke is saying. The half a cheese sandwich is gone, and an afternoon's work awaits. "Do the job every day, get in your car, and go home. Keep your ass out of the clubhouse. Stay away from locker rooms. Avoid group thinking and individuals with low self-esteem."

As we listen to Jack Burke Junior, in person or in his books, we should remember to stop and be amazed. He spans centuries, and eras, and yet is younger in intellect and vigor than lots of people half his age. He's strong enough to command your attention with a squeeze or a poke or pop. But what is perhaps most likeable about him is that he's opinionated enough for great conversation while not coming off as a know-it-all. Burke allows disagreement. He's a leader, not a dictator. Now that's a good dad.

10

BACK TO THE *MARIPOSAS*

Avery and Gilbert Freeman

The bamboo suspension bridges at Club de Golf Covadonga sag at the ends and wiggle in the middle, making a crossing feel like a particularly difficult field sobriety test. So you throw out your arms like a tightrope walker and try not to look down into the muddy tributary of the Río Valles six feet below.

Covadonga and its thrilling bridges doze in a clearing in the rainforest between Tampico and Mexico City. Its holes are nine tunnels in the jungle, its greens putt like shag carpets saturated with honey, and the indispensable tool of the grounds crew is the machete. An air of mystery and secrecy pervades the place. There's not a word about it on the Web, in phone directories, or in history books. Even people in the nearest town, Ciudad Valles, swear it no longer exists. Yet despite its crumbling concrete entryway, and the gray-green moss and peeling paint on its eerie, abandoned hotel, Covadonga lives. But barely. Although it is the

above: AVERY FREEMAN, WITH MUNDO.

only course in a seventy-five-mile radius, tourists can't find it, and only forty members pay the 600 peso (about $55) monthly dues. Its pro shop holds a pro, Andres Morales, but no shop.

What Covadonga has in abundance, however, is *mariposas.* Butterflies. Butterflies are what brought Gilbert Freeman to this place every summer when he was a kid. And butterflies took the Lakewood (Dallas) Country Club pro back this winter for the first time in thirty-two years.

Avery Freeman, Gilbert's father, was the Tiger Woods of lepidoptery. "Few individuals in recent decades can match his contributions," writes Andrew D. Warren of Oregon State University. "Our current knowledge of Mexican *hesperiid* diversity is based on his groundbreaking research . . . The excitement generated in the community of North American lepidopterists by Avery's early publications on *Megathymini* cannot be overstated." Living on grant money from such as the National Geographic Society, the Smithsonian, and the Carnegie Institute, and driving a stick-shift Chevy station wagon, the biology teacher at Hillcrest High in Dallas collected widely and well on his annual haj to South Texas and Mexico. A meticulous and thorough scientist, he identified 107 new species during his career—so many that he could afford a little whimsy when asserting the discoverer's right to assign a Latin name. He named three butterflies for his wife, Louise, including *Megathymus yuccae louiseae;* one each for daughters Linda (*Amblyscirtes linda*) and Julia (*Lerodea julia*); and two for his son, Gilbert (*Astraptes gilberti* and *Agathymus gilberti*). Even his Covadonga caddie, Benito Reycendes, was bestowed a piece of obscure immortality (*Poanes benito*).

During the family's fourth summer at Covadonga, thirteen-year-old Gilbert discovered the game they played on the nine-hole course outside the hotel. Almost immediately, he put down his net, and golf became to him what butterflies were to his father. Gilbert played every day and entered his stats and a succinct analysis in a diary ("hit number four in two but bogied five *again!*"), mimicking his father's careful end-of-the-day notations in his butterfly logbook. His parents took up the game the following year, and summertime acquired a pleasing rhythm: golf at dawn; butterfly stalking for father, precisely one hundred practice shots for his son; lunch and a siesta during the hottest part of the day; more butterflies and practice balls; and then, for all three, a final nine holes before dinner. The best days of their lives, they all say.

Louise Freeman can close her eyes, she says, and see her husband disappear into the jungle to the right of the ninth fairway, looking simultaneously gentle and fierce, with a long-handled net in one hand and a machete in the other. Avery Freeman had a mustache, large, luminous brown eyes like his son, and leather boots laced up to the knee to protect against snakes.

In February 2006, Gilbert returned to Covadonga. He carried his father's ashes in a black Hogan shag bag.

Gilbert had never been to Mexico in the cool part of the year. He remembers only summer in the jungle, when heat attacked in shimmering waves and big hats and siestas were more a necessity than a choice. But his father never rested long after lunch; the flapping of butterfly wings kept him from dozing. So while the others slept in hammocks or on rumpled sheets, with ceiling fans turning lazily over their heads, he'd be lacing his boots and checking his pockets for the little waxed paper envelopes he used to store specimens. He'd grab a net and his jungle knife and out he'd go.

"The best collecting is to be done around the irrigation ditches and canals and along the Rio Grande River," Avery wrote in the *Journal of the Lepidopterists' Society* of a 1960 trip to the Tex-Mex borderland. "One of the best places to collect was found to be on the La Reforma ranch . . . Any person desiring to find this locality can get there by driving from Hidalgo alongside the railroad and turn left on the dirt road that has a high power line running parallel to it . . ." Gilbert would have been five years old when this adventure took place, and, as his mother recalls, he was there.

In the '60s, as their youngest child got older and more adaptable, the Freemans ventured farther and farther south, past the giant hook of the Yucatán Peninsula all the way to Guatemala and Belize. Their Spanish improved, and they got to know where to get a Coke or a *cerveza* in a variety of exotic locations – Veracruz, Tamazunchale, Tabasco, Oaxaca. For years they rolled through Mexico in a rust-colored '63 wagon, then a yellow '67 with a black interior. Neither had air-conditioning, because Avery didn't trust the technology. Despite the skin-adhering vinyl coverings and the noise from the open windows, Gilbert loved that yellow car. Its rear-facing back seat allowed him to alternately watch the wild country recede and to look down to read the science fiction that was his addiction. Isaac Asimov, Ray Bradbury . . . Robert Heinlein's *Stranger in a Strange Land* was one of his favorites. Wrapped in reverie, Gilbert felt like the king of the road.

"We'd stop anywhere, at any time, and Dad would grab his

net and disappear for an hour," he recalls. When the father returned to the car, his son helped locate the cigar boxes in which they stored the dramatically colored, recently deceased *mariposas.* "I was really into all the things my dad did," Gilbert says. "I was sure I was going to be a scientist like him, probably an archaeologist." He got an A on every science project and the subject of every project was butterflies – their migration, their anatomy, the beautiful miracle of their existence.

Then golf happened. Gilbert and Louise learned in the usual way, with a little professional instruction and practice. Not Avery. Back home in Garland, the middle-aged biology teacher applied the scientific method to the project, testing various swing hypotheses by endlessly hitting whiffle golf balls against the house. *Whack*-thump. *Whack*-thump. *Whack*-thump. Torture for people inside: "*A*-very!" Louise would yell. "Could you please stop that racket! And look what you're doing to the lawn!"

Despite the thorough experimentation, Avery Freeman's swing remained a faintly agricultural chop, as if he were holding a machete and not a five iron. He had a too-strong grip and a short game that could explode at any minute. No lessons – he didn't believe in the technology. He got the job as the Hillcrest High golf coach, and kept it for ten years, but the resultant proximity to golfers and golf courses didn't help his own game much. He shot a 39 for nine holes once, at Eastern Hills in Garland – his high-water mark. Usually, he was all bogies.

At age eighteen, Gilbert stopped going on the trip to Covadonga. He had a bigtime junior golf career going by this time, with college coaches wanting to give him a scholarship, and a job in the bag room at Dallas Athletic Club. Father and son enjoyed golf separately from then on, unless Gilbert had a tournament, when Avery would watch quietly, stealthily, as if he were hunting something.

That first summer Gilbert didn't accompany his parents to the jungle, he planned a small party for the night before their return. Three of his buddies and their four dates convened at the Freeman house before going to a concert at Fair Park Coliseum, near the Cotton Bowl in Dallas. They'd be grooving to West Coast funk band Tower of Power ("What Is Hip?" was one of their hits). Rare Earth was the headliner, six slightly psychedelic boys from Chicago who sang "Get Ready." The young men at the party wore Izod shirts, designer jeans, and hair that spilled halfway down foreheads and over ears. The girls had slithered into the same brands of fancy pants as the boys. Their hair was Big: curling irons and hairspray allowed them to form the center-parted, gravity-defying 'do of actress Farah Fawcett. There may have been beer cans scattered about the Freeman house in suburban Dallas that night, and the phone may have been pulled out of the wall; Gilbert is a little hazy on those details. But he's quite clear that the music was loud and that the carpet bore a new stain from spilled Pace Picante.

He's also definite – this he can't forget – that suddenly, shockingly, a full day earlier than expected, his parents walked in. Avery and Louise hugged their son and didn't make a scene. They just told the kids to have a good time and to be careful.

But they were waiting up when Gilbert came home. Despite all the summers of bonding in the jungle, and their son's newfound maturity, the chain of command was never in doubt.

. . .

Gilbert travels back to Mexico with an odd feeling of excitement and nostalgia. Behind the wheel of a rented Suburban, he observes dogs aimlessly wandering the streets of the muddy little towns between Tampico and Valles. There are speed bumps instead of traffic lights, and open-air grills emanating delicious smells. A funeral halts traffic. The coffin is on a pickup truck and a few score of mourners follow it on foot. A mother wheels her small child on a dolly, like a mover. The people on the street stare at the pale faces in our car. We stare back.

"It's like hunting any other animal," Freeman explains during the two-hour, seventy-five-mile drive. "Skippers are *real* fast. You sneak up from behind, get them in your net, then flip it, quickly, so they can't fly out again. Then you've got to kill them right away, to keep them from beating their wings up."

Skippers are what?

"Slightly smaller butterflies, with different veins in their wings and different antennae."

And you kill them how?

"You pinch their necks. There's an art to it."

While Freeman drives, one of his fellow travelers, Dan Strimple, another Dallas-based golf pro, tries to form his first-ever Spanish phrases. Strimple tends to wing it when he's out of his element, so he's thrilled to discover that a number of Spanish words can be formed by simply adding an *a* or an *o* to the English word: *crédito, cemento, sexo.*

"How do you say, 'I want'?" Strimple asks. "How do you say, 'with you'?"

He digests for a moment, then: "*Yo quiero sexo con usted.*"

In Valles, Freeman turns south on Ruta 85, passing a huge

statue of Emiliano Zapata. Dodging speeding trucks comically overloaded with sugar cane, he drives unerringly to this place he used to know but now doesn't. Covadonga's face has changed beyond imagining, like a long-lost friend who has let himself go. PROPIEDAD FEDERAL, a sign says – what the hell does that mean? He creeps the car along a dark, primeval path. "Jeez," Gilbert mutters. "Wow." Tree branches with big white flowers scratch the sides of the car and saplings tickle it underneath. The hotel is a phantom amid the aggressive jungle. At the end of the path is Andres Morales, the caddie who never left, now the pro.

"Heel-bare?" he says. "I can't believe you're here."

They hug. *¿Benito está aquí?* No – Gilbert's caddie, a rough man who was never without his white straw cowboy hat and a burning cigarette, is dead. Too much *cerveza,* too much *fumar,* Andres explains. And Mundo? No, *lo siento* – sorry – Avery Freeman's caddie also is *muerto.* But Raymundo, Gilbert's mother's caddie, the credit manager at the Ford dealership in Valles, has been alerted by cell phone of the miraculous appearance of "Heel-bare," and in a few moments, he pulls up on his motorcycle. They exchange hugs and laughter. Back in the day, Raymundo would find tees to match the color of Louise Freeman's outfits, and hand her a color-coordinated peg with her driver. His English was and remains excellent; he wrote the Freemans a letter every year at Christmas.

Green parrots screech in the giant India Laurel above our heads, and the conversation stops. Andres observes the sadness in Gilbert's eyes: is it the death of the caddies, or the fingers of rust and rot grasping the once white clubhouse, or the bamboo and palms trying to suffocate the hotel? "Covadonga," Andres says softly. "Almost gone."

The last part of a butterfly's four-stage life, the flying part, usually lasts only a week or two. A generation of butterflies is called a flight. In the tropics, in the summer, there is flight after flight, and death and life mingle constantly.

Every butterfly meal is sipped through the straw of its proboscis, and every species will take nectar or the juice from rotting fruit if it can get it. Plenty of both at Covadonga: along its fairways grow mangoes, bananas, lemons, and limes. The jungle has taken over the orange grove by nine but still, no caddie or butterfly ever goes hungry.

And no golfer feels bored. You're stymied from the tee on both the par threes, with a three iron in your hands. Virile trees virtually surround the green of the mystifying fifth, a 234-yard par four from the back tee (only Andres has the proper shot – a karate chop with a laminated Stan Thompson six wood). The bunker sand is not sand but – this is only a theory – the stuff the ants throw out when they dig their homes. And to say the greens are slow really doesn't capture the feeling. They are glacial. They are an old man walking uphill underwater in lead boots. The ball rolls on them as if it were a wet sponge. In short, it's a course to make you grit your teeth, especially when the local experts – Andres, Raymundo, and a part-time caddie named Luis – are kicking your ass. Even after playing it for three days, Covadonga remains an insolvable puzzle, like chess in the dark.

But Strimple will not allow anything but laughter. More *cerveza*, he says at lunch, then more. When someone notices how the sunscreen on his face contrasts with his pink skin, he begins to call himself El Diablo Blanco. "How do you do," he says in his awful pidgin to a new, very surprised-looking acquaintance. "I'm the Devil." At a bar, in keeping with his vowelization of English to make, he hopes, Spanish, he asks for a glass of Coca-Cola with "rum-a." At a party in honor of the Americans under twinkling Christmas lights in the front yard at la casa de Andres Morales in Valles, El Diablo Blanco declares the whole thing—the food and the drinks and the golf course and the company—to be "awesome-miento." Most of all, Strimple the morale officer keeps an eye on Gilbert. Is his friend feeling his father, gone now for four years, or for his youth, gone now for much longer? And when, and where, will he spread his father's ashes?

On the morning of the third day, when Gilbert carries his clubs to the first tee, he's got the black Hogan shag bag in his left hand.

He nails his tee shot—he's an excellent player; he twice qualified for the Byron Nelson Classic, a PGA Tour event—but he doesn't leave the tee right away. He hangs back, and walks slowly to the dark jungle thicket to the right of the first fairway. He opens the bag and opens his hand. Some of the ashes of Avery Freeman hang in the air.

Gilbert repeats this ceremony a few more times, and we leave him alone. Luis, who putts like a safe cracker and has the strongest grip on the planet, knows what's going on. He talks for a minute about fatherhood, and his own father. He and his wife Maribel have only two *niñas*, he says, Karla and Zaira. His own padre was much more prolific, fathering eight boys consecutively, then five girls in a row. The twelve siblings of Luis talk about his small output, he says with a smile. That's one of his brothers over there, Magda, the man with a gray mustache and a rake standing by the creek in front of the fourth green. Magda has six children. The Martínez brothers smile at each other and wave.

"I go twice to United States for work, *cemento,* and use that to buy the, the, *terra*? – the land – for my house. I build the house." To make ends meet when he's not carrying a bag at Covadonga, Luis tends bar in Valles.

After this, our final round, we all walk through the abandoned hotel, the empty, echoing space that was Gilbert's home for eight summers. That was the bowling alley, Gilbert says – two lanes. I used to skateboard down that ramp. I hung my hammock on those hooks. My father used to come in here for a Covadonga cocktail, which was red. There were snakeskins on the wall, there and there.

No guests have checked in since the early '80s, Andres explains. That was when the government decided that Covadonga should be the center of a giant lake. The administration paid off the owner – a Spanish guy, according to Andres – and condemned the place. Then a new group came to power in Mexico City and forgot the lake idea. And that's why, says Andres, we're left with – this.

Gilbert gives Luis his watch, and Andres his clubs, dozens of golf balls, gloves, golf towels – almost enough to stock his shop. *Hasta luego, amigo, hasta luego* . . . As the car threads through the crooked path to the highway, Gilbert isn't sure if the pleasure of the last few days has outweighed the pain; it has seemed at times that the fun from the golf and the reunions had only sharpened a dormant sadness. Yet he had come close to crying only once, when he carried the shag bag to the jungle bordering the ninth fairway and scattered the last of Avery's ashes. But at that moment the son thought that his dad would live on, in a way, in this out-of-the-way place. As a butterfly floating over slow greens.

ACKNOWLEDGMENTS

I would like to acknowledge Susan Canavan of Houghton Mifflin—a wonderful editor—and Byrd Leavell of Scott Waxman Literary—a great agent; Lisa Glover, for her copyediting, and Lisa Diercks, for designing a beautiful book: Thank you. Thank you very much. I also owe a debt of gratitude to the following books and people:

CHAPTER 2: DADDY CADDIE

A New History of Korea by Ki-baik Lee. Translated by Edward W. Wagner and Edward J. Schultz (Harvard University Press, Cambridge, MA: 1984)

Life of Beethoven by Ates Orga (Paganiniana Publications, Neptune City, NJ: 1980)

—*With thanks to Pat Madden*

CHAPTER 3: $227.05

—*With thanks to Marty Leonard*

CHAPTER 4: ULSTERMEN

The God Delusion by Richard Dawkins (Houghton Mifflin, Boston: 2007)

The Truth About the Irish by Terry Eagleton (St. Martin's Griffin, New York: 1999)

—*With thanks to Steve Sampson and Julianne B. Arnold*

CHAPTER 7: FAR

Buried Lies by Peter Jacobsen with Jack Sheehan (G. P. Putnam's Sons, New York: 1993)

Embedded Balls by Peter Jacobsen with Jack Sheehan (G. P. Putnam's Sons, New York: 2005)

– With thanks to Joyle Dahl, Jim French, Robert Tennant, and Pat Becker

CHAPTER 8: DON'T HIT THIS CLUB UNLESS YOU'VE GOT FIVE HUNDRED DOLLARS

They Call Me Super Mex by Lee Trevino and Sam Blair (Random House, New York: 1982)

– With thanks to Sam Blair

CHAPTER 9: OUR FATHER

Ten Lessons in Golf by Jack Burke (Brown and Bigelow, Saint Paul: 1921)

It's Only a Game by Jack Burke Junior (Gotham Books, New York: 2006)

– With thanks to Bill Earley